Cooking for an
ALLERGY-FREE
lifestyle

Cooking for an
ALLERGY-FREE
lifestyle

Tammi Forman

Styling by Brita du Plessis

Photography by Matthys van Lill

Published in 2010 by Struik Lifestyle
(an imprint of Random House Struik (Pty) Ltd)
Company Reg. No. 1966/003153/07
80 McKenzie Street, Cape Town 8001
PO Box 1144, Cape Town, 8000, South Africa

Copyright © in published edition:
Random House Struik (Pty) Ltd 2010
Copyright © in text: Tammi Forman 2010
Copyright © in photographs:
Random House Struik (Pty) Ltd 2010

www.randomstruik.co.za

Publisher: Linda de Villiers
Managing editor: Cecilia Barfield
Editor and indexer: Bronwen Leak
Designer: Helen Henn
Photographer: Matthys van Lill
Food stylist: Brita du Plessis
Stylist's assistant: Yvette Pascoe
Proofreader: Gill Gordon

Reproduction: Hirt & Carter Cape (Pty) Ltd
Printing and binding: Times Offset (M) Sdn Bhd

ISBN 978-1-77007-899-4

The publishers wish to thank Nap Interiors for the loan of
props for the photography.

www.imagesofafrica.co.za

IMAGES OF AFRICA
PHOTO LIBRARY

Over 40 000 unique African images available to purchase
from our image bank at www.imagesofafrica.co.za

Acknowledgements

A word of thanks ...

With grateful thanks to G-d for the 'strength' to write this book. To my husband, partner, best friend and love – Larry, who truly stands by me through thick and thin and is always available to taste test – honestly! To all the people who have contributed ideas and recipes for me to tweak into allergy-friendly versions. To my mom and dad for all their encouragement. To my sister, Jacqui, for all her help with ingredients, encouragement and training. To Patricia for helping me with all the prep with a smile on her face! And most importantly, to my Inspirations – Joey, Lennie and Sam – my three precious gifts for whom this book was written. The idea to publish it came a long time after I began compiling the recipes for YOU. Boys, your gratitude for my efforts and enthusiasm for my inventions keeps me inspired to keep at it.

Contents

Foreword

There is no discounting the importance of adequate or ideally optimal nutrition for every person. It is crucial for the growth and development of children as well as for disease prevention, vitality and longevity in both kids and adults. Frequently though, these principles get set aside when a family faces the risks associated with allergies in a family member. It can be overwhelming and it is most definitely frightening. An allergic person cannot 'take a chance' of being mistakenly exposed to an offending food, often even in the most minute quantities. Although almost any food can trigger an allergic reaction or intolerance, the most common offenders are peanuts and tree nuts, eggs, fish and seafood, milk protein, wheat, soy and strawberries, as well as food additives and colourings. Exposure to food allergens can cause a range of symptoms from headaches, fatigue and discomfort to rashes, hives and anaphalactic shock. The reaction is usually swift and requires medical attention, often urgently.

Each year more and more people are diagnosed with allergies as well as intolerances to food. This amounts to millions of adults and children. It is, therefore, no surprise that you either have an allergy yourself or have a family member or friend who does.

Imagine life without ever having bread, breakfast cereal, cakes and biscuits or any other treats. Sounds dull and isolating doesn't it? Well, this finely researched and fabulous book will guide you through restoring a healthy balance into your life and will return the fun of eating and socialising to those allergic kids and adults, their families and friends. The recipes are quick and easy, and use common and easy to acquire ingredients. There are often variations to the recipes, allowing you to tailor-make the item according to your specific requirements.

No longer is bread and cake never allowed. As long as the required substitutions – which are clearly marked in the book – are followed, you can enjoy a party or a healthy home-cooked meal, as well as a snack. The tips spread throughout the book for normalising occasions despite the allergy are fantastic. This piece of work is invaluable. It is what we have all been waiting for. I trust it will be as useful and enjoyable to you as it is for me.

NICKI URISON
Registered Dietician (South Africa)

Foreword

True food allergy should not be confused with the many other causes of reactions to food.

A true food allergy always involves the immune system and is measurable when it involves the Immunoglobulin E [IgE] part of the immune system. This is an overreaction of the immune system rather than a lack. This IgE is measurable by a RAST blood test (radioallergosorbent test). True food allergy can range from a mild condition to that of a life-threatening episode. Non-IgE food allergy is possible and an example of this is gluten sensitivity. Other causes of reactions to food include food intolerance (no known immune mechanism), enzyme deficiencies, toxins, food additives and chemicals.

When possible, avoiding the offending food is advisable. Sometimes avoidance can be difficult, either because the food is very common or because too many foods are involved. When multiple foods are involved, complete avoidance can sometimes leave the child worse off as a consequence of an unbalanced diet. It is important to correctly identify offending foods and this should be done with the help of scientifically centered medical personnel. Importantly, children placed on elimination diets should always have the uninvolved foods reintroduced to the daily diet so that they do not inadvertently starve.

With this background, please use the recipes before you with as much joy and pleasure as I know the author has done.

DR ALLAN S PUTERMAN
MBChB (UCT)
Fellow of the College of Paediatricians of South Africa
Fellow of the American Academy of Allergy Asthma and Immunology

'I don't skate to where the puck is, I skate to where the puck will be.'

WAYNE GRETSKEY [ICE HOCKEY CHAMPION]

Introduction

This is a recipe book with a difference. It is written by a person with allergies, for people with allergies, but the recipes it contains are as delicious as any dairy-laden, wheat-ridden or egg-loaded dishes. Most importantly, this book is for easy cooking. It is not an exercise in paint-by-numbers: it offers guidelines for you to add and take away, and mix and match to create your own original. My aim is that you don't spend hours in the kitchen cooking, yet still produce allergy-friendly, delicious foods.

My name is Tammi. I'm 40, married (to Larry) and have three great sons: Joey, aged eleven, Lennie, aged ten, and Sam, aged seven. My career journey began as an artist and fashion designer. Marriage, and then children, shifted my focus and I was no longer drawn to fashion design. I decided to take some time off to be a mom. During this period, we immigrated to Seattle, USA and emigrated back to Cape Town, South Africa. I taught preschool, ran summer camps and, in-between, encountered some major allergy issues.

I have a sensitivity to wheat and sugar. Then along came my first-born, Joey, who was breastfed but still managed to suffer from wheat and dairy issues (with some mould and dust-mite sensitivities thrown in too). Lennie, who came second, had to avoid wheat and dairy ... okay, now add (actually take away) orange, pineapple, kiwi, strawberry, white potato (no chips!), tomato, peppers, aubergine ... and anything including these items. A few years on came Sam ... egg, soya, dairy, wheat, nuts, peanuts (don't worry, we're doing better – he can now have wheat and soy) ... and all of these with the threat of anaphylactic shock hanging over our heads. Heavens, you say, what did they eat? Good question, because with all the processed food around, they still manage to eat a ton of wonderful food.

I want to share our family secrets and recipes with you because I know how hard it is to be 'alone' with allergies – your own or your children's; to not be able to eat what other people are eating; to be afraid to send your children to places where they might encounter a substance that seems so innocuous to others, but that could be fatal to them; to be judged 'difficult' or 'weird' by others who don't understand why you can't just do what everyone else is doing. Well, there are ways to be able to have your cake (even if it is wheat/egg/dairy-free) and eat it too. This book makes it easy and shows how my family, with all our weird and wonderful allergies, lives a normal life. People often stare at me in disbelief and pity: You can't have x and y and z and more? Well, this book is filled with yummy foods and gives alternatives that are easy and delicious.

Food is the very first pleasure we experience. The preparation of food is an act of love – the sharing of it with family and friends, its consummation. The main ingredients for successful cooking are enthusiasm, perseverance, a spirit of adventure and the anticipation of joy. These ingredients are essential to every recipe. Having said this, you need a well-organised and well-stocked pantry too!

I am a firm believer in being organised. When you're baking a batch, bake two and freeze one for those last-minute play-dates, school lunches, etc. Have a few extra casseroles and soups in the freezer. Wheat-free breads freeze well and save you the schlep when you can't just pop in to your local café to buy a loaf – I know it saves my sanity over and over again! Having a stock of items is insurance against having to rush out and buy an exorbitantly expensive ready-made item (like wheat-free biscuits), and allows you to always have an alternative at hand for those one or two children who can't have x, y or z.

This is a highly practical book, with emphasis on convenience and quality of cooking. We live in the age of information. Despite its many benefits, we sometimes find it difficult to distinguish the practical, useful ideas amidst the flood with which we are constantly bombarded. I hope that this book provides clarity in the 'how to' of living a balanced and affordable allergy-friendly lifestyle! By returning to the basics, and simplifying our choices (and our recipes), we can eat delicious food that maintains our good health ... and not go broke or crazy in the process!

TAMMI FORMAN

Substitutes

You've lived a perfectly 'normal' life when, suddenly, out jumps an annoying little alien called Allergy or Sensitivity. This section will help you to use your original recipes that you know and love and just replace the 'offenders'.

Below you will find a list of allergens and their substitutes:

Allergen	Substitute
cow's milk	almond/coconut/goat's/rice/soy milk
cow's milk cheese	goat's milk/soy cheese
cow's milk yoghurt	goat's milk/soy yoghurt
eggs (whole or albumen)	Orgran No Egg powder OR, in baking, 1 tsp vinegar = 1 egg
gluten flour, e.g. wheat, rye, barley, oat	chickpea/cornflour/millet/rice/soy flour
mayonnaise	egg-free mayonnaise (e.g. From Mommy with Love, All Joy)
wheat bread	100% rye bread/rice cakes/corn thins/Finn Crisp crackers
wheat flour	barley/rye flour

Wheat-free and gluten-free flours

People often ask me: Does X (i.e. rye) contain wheat? (The answer is no.) Wheat flour contains gluten, which is the protein that strengthens and binds dough in baking. Because of this, when baking with non-wheat flours, you may need to source alternative binding agents. Wheat-free recipes using flour substitutes usually have been carefully formulated to get the best possible result by taking into account the problems associated with a lack of wheat gluten. Substitution can, therefore, be a risky experiment. If you try substitution, then be aware that you may end up with a taste that differs from the usual 'wheat taste' you expected – so don't do it for the first time if cooking for an important occasion!

The flours that follow are alternatives to wheat flour. However, it is important to be aware that there is no exact substitute for wheat flour and recipes made with wheat-free alternative flours will be different from those containing wheat.

Amaranth flour is made from the seed of the Amaranth plant, which is a leafy vegetable. Amaranth seeds are very high in protein, which makes this a nutritious flour for baking. Alternative names: African spinach, Chinese spinach, Indian spinach, elephant's ear

✓ Wheat free | ✓ Gluten free

Arrowroot flour is ground from the root of the plant and is very useful for thickening recipes. It tastes a little like liquorice and the fine powder becomes clear when it is cooked, which makes it ideal for thickening clear sauces.

✓ Wheat free | ✓ Gluten free

Barley flour only contains a small amount of gluten, so it is rarely used alone to make bread. It has a slightly nutty flavour and can be used to thicken or flavour soups or stews. Blended with other alternative flours it is also fairly versatile for cakes, biscuits, pastry, dumplings, etc.

✓ Wheat free | ✗ Gluten free

Buckwheat flour is not, despite its name, a form of wheat. Buckwheat is actually related to rhubarb. The small seeds of the plant are ground to make flour. It has a strong nutty taste so is not generally used on its own in a recipe, as the taste of the finished product can be very overpowering and a little bitter. Buckwheat grains cook up as a delicious alternative to rice. Alternative names: beech wheat, kasha, saracen corn

✓ Wheat free | ✓ Gluten free

Chickpea flour is ground from chickpeas and has a strong, slightly nutty taste. It is not generally used on its own. Combine it with rice and maize flour for bread or biscuit baking. Alternative names: gram flour, garbanzo flour

✓ Wheat free | ✓ Gluten free

Cornflour is milled from corn (maize) into a fine, white powder and is used for thickening recipes and sauces. It has a bland taste and is therefore used in conjunction with other ingredients that will impart flavour to the recipe. It also works very well when mixed with other flours, for example when making fine batters. Some types of cornflour are milled from wheat, but are labelled wheaten cornflour and are not suitable for people with a gluten allergy. Alternative name: cornstarch

✓ Wheat free | ✓ Gluten free

Cornmeal or polenta is ground from corn. Heavier than cornflour, it has a grainy, gritty texture and is blended with other flours. It is good in breads.

✓ Wheat free | ✓ Gluten free

Maize flour is ground from corn. It is heavier than cornflour.

✓ Wheat free | ✓ Gluten free

Millet flour comes from the grass family and is used as a cereal in many African and Asian countries. It can be used to thicken soups and make flat breads and griddle cakes. Because it lacks any form of gluten it's not suitable for many types of baking.

✓ Wheat free | ✓ Gluten free

Potato flour should not be confused with potato starch flour. Potato flour has a strong potato flavour and is a heavy flour, so a little goes a long way. Bulk buying is not recommended unless you are using it on a regular basis for a variety of recipes, as it does not have a very long shelf life.

✓ Wheat free | ✓ Gluten free

Potato starch flour is a fine white flour made from potatoes. It has a light potato flavour that is undetectable when used in recipes. It's one of the few alternative flours that keeps very well, provided it is stored in an airtight jar, somewhere cool and dark.

✓ Wheat free | ✓ Gluten free

Quinoa grain or flour, pronounced 'keen wa', is related to the plant family of spinach and beets. It has been used for over 5 000 years as a cereal. The Incas called it the 'mother seed'. Quinoa provides a good source of vegetable protein and it is the seeds of the quinoa plant that are ground to make flour. The flour has a stronger flavour and taste than the grain and is best used in combination with other flours. It's a rarity to find quinoa flour, although quinoa itself is widely available.

✓ Wheat free | ✓ Gluten free

Rice flour, brown is heavier than its relative, white rice flour. It is milled from unpolished brown rice so it has a higher nutritional value than white and, as it contains the bran of the brown rice, it has a higher fibre content. This also means that it is a bit grainy. It does have a slight nutty taste, which will sometimes come out in recipes depending on the other ingredients, and the texture will also contribute to a heavier product than recipes made with white rice flour. It is not often used completely on its own, because of its heavier nature. Bulk buying is not recommended as it is better used when fresh.

✓ Wheat free | ✓ Gluten free

Rice flour, white is milled from polished white rice, so it is very bland in taste and not particularly nutritious. White rice flour is ideal for recipes that require a light texture. It can be used on its own for a variety of recipes and has a reasonable shelf life, as long as it is stored in an airtight container to avoid it absorbing moisture from the air.

✓ Wheat free | ✓ Gluten free

Rye flour is a strongly flavoured flour, dark in colour. Breads made with rye flour are denser than those made with wheat, for example pumpernickel, which is virtually black. Rye flour has a low gluten content, but it can be used for baking things like pancakes and muffins, as well as breads.

✓ Wheat free | ✗ Gluten free

Sorghum meal is relatively difficult to find, but 'Maltabella' porridge, in its raw form, can be used. It is ground from sorghum grain, which is similar to millet. This dark coloured flour/meal is used to make porridge or flat unleavened breads. It can also be used in combination in breads. Sorghum flour has a pleasant smell as well as taste. It is an important staple in Africa and India.

✓ Wheat free | ✓ Gluten free

Soya flour is a high-protein flour with a nutty taste. It is not generally used on its own in recipes, but when combined with other flours is very successful as an alternative flour. It can be used to thicken recipes or added as a flavour enhancer. It needs to be carefully stored as it is has a high fat content and can go rancid if not stored properly. A cool, dark environment is recommended. It can even be stored in the refrigerator.

✓ Wheat free | ✓ Gluten free

Tapioca flour is made from the root of the cassava plant. Once ground, it takes the form of a light, soft, fine white flour. Tapioca flour adds chewiness to baking and is a good thickener. Although difficult to source, it is an excellent addition to any wheat-free kitchen. It can be made by milling the tapioca grain. It's a fairly resilient flour, so storing at room temperature is no problem.

✓ Wheat free | ✓ Gluten free

Teff flour is made from Teff, which comes from the grass family and is a tiny cereal grain native to northern Africa. It is ground into flour and used to prepare injera, a spongy, slightly sour flatbread. It is now finding a niche in the health-food market, because it is very nutritious, although currently it's a rarity in South Africa.

✓ Wheat free | ✓ Gluten free

KEY

alt	alternatively
DF	dairy free
EF	egg free
GF	gluten free
NF	nut free
SF	sugar free
WF	wheat free
YF	yeast free
½ tsp	2.5 ml
1 tsp	5 ml
1 Tbsp	15 ml
¼ cup	60 ml
⅓ cup	80 ml
½ cup	125 ml
1 cup	250 ml

The key explained: **WF; GF; NF; alt DF**
As an example, the Wheat-free crustless quiche (page 56) is wheat free, gluten free and nut free. If, however, you substitute the cow's milk for soy milk (indicated as an alternative in the ingredients list), the recipe will be dairy free as well.

Vegan pancakes (front, page 20)
Banana muffins (back, page 17)

'When you wake up in the morning, Pooh,' said Piglet at last, 'what's the first thing you say to yourself?'
'What's for breakfast?' said Pooh. 'What do you say, Piglet?'
'I say, I wonder what's going to happen exciting today?' said Piglet.
Pooh nodded thoughtfully. 'It's the same thing,' he said.

A.A. Milne, *The House at Pooh Corner*

Healthy *breakfasts*

In our home, a 'happy' breakfast is just as important as a healthy one; it starts the day off 'right'. We each have different tastes and Sammy, the most different of us all, often asks for a 'meal', meaning last night's supper leftovers.

Sunday mornings are spent over a leisurely breakfast with a delicious cup of freshly brewed filter coffee or two. Our boys prefer a pot of 'Pooh bear honey tea' (rooibos made with honey), so named by Joey as a toddler, to accompany their choices.

Whatever breakfast you prefer, whether a muffin on the run, a smoothie or a 'meal' – take the time to eat one, it really IS the most important meal of your day.

Magic mix breakfast cereal

This cereal gives a slow energy release that keeps you 'full' and focused for longer, due to stable blood-sugar levels. This makes it excellent for people with ADD, diabetes and cholesterol.

2 cups rolled oats
1 cup oat bran
½–1 cup desiccated coconut (optional)
½ cup sunflower seeds
½ cup pumpkin seeds
½–1 cup linseeds/flax seeds
½ cup sesame seeds (optional)
½ cup seedless raisins

½ cup dried cranberries
½ cup chopped dried apple or mango pieces (optional)
2 cups cornflakes or Oatees or Rice Krispies
a handful of raw almonds (optional)
½ cup dry soy/rice/cow's milk powder for a protein boost (optional)

1. Mix everything together and store in an airtight container. It won't last long before it's all 'yummed' up!
2. For kids, the addition of regular cereals makes it 'OK' and they love the dried fruit. We change the ingredients slightly each time for variation.
3. Serve with warm or cold rice, soy or cow's milk or plain yoghurt.

WF; EF; SF; YF; alt GF; alt NF; alt DF | Makes 14–18 servings

Sundaes on Sunday

½ cup magic mix breakfast cereal (see above) or granola (see page 17)
½ cup plain or fruit-flavoured yoghurt

fresh fruit (bananas, mangoes, strawberries, figs, gooseberries, etc.)
honey to taste

1. Presentation goes a long way. Half-fill a sundae or medium hi-ball glass with the cereal. Top with the yoghurt, slice some fresh fruit on top and drizzle with honey. Serve with a long-handled teaspoon.

EF; WF; alt GF; alt NF | Serves 1

TIP: For an extra-special treat, top with ice cream or banana frozen dessert (see page 77).

Sensational smoothies

These are good not only for breakfast, but also for lunch in summer when it's just too hot for a cooked breakfast.

1 cup rice/soy/almond/coconut/goat's/cow's
   milk or yoghurt
1 Tbsp oat bran
3 ice cubes (optional)

Choose 2–3 fruit combinations:
1 sliced banana
½ cup strawberries
½ cup blueberries
½ cup raspberries (fresh or frozen)
½ cup orange juice
1 fresh sliced mango

Add
1–2 Tbsp seed mix (flax, sesame, sunflower,
   pumpkin) or 10 walnuts/cashews/pecans/
   almonds (optional)

Treat extras
a drizzle of honey
a chunk of carob
a sprinkle of chocolate chips

1. Place all your ingredients in a blender and blend until smooth. Serve in a tall glass, drizzled with honey. It's a delicious and refreshing meal in a glass.

WF; EF; GF; alt DF; alt NF | Serves 1

Chocolate oats

It's healthier than it sounds! I love this delicious winter breakfast.

1 cup soy/rice/cow's milk
1 tsp cocoa powder (Bournville is
   my favourite)
1 Tbsp fructose or sugar

½ cup rolled oats
1 Tbsp chocolate or carob chips
honey to taste

1. In a pot over a medium heat, warm the milk. Do not boil.
2. Add the cocoa powder and stir until dissolved.
3. Add the fructose or sugar, followed by the oats. Stir until cooked.
4. Spoon into a bowl, sprinkle with chocolate or carob chips and drizzle with honey.

WF; NF; alt DF; alt SF | Serves 1

TIP: Add a diced apple, sliced banana, handful of almonds or 1 Tbsp oat bran for extra fibre.

Granola

250 g margarine or 1 cup sunflower oil	**Optional extras** (add to mix before baking)
2 cups sugar or 1½ cups fructose	½ cup sunflower seeds
4 cups oats	½ cup sesame seeds
2 cups flour (choose from a combination of rice, rye, barley and sorghum)	1 cup flaked almonds
1–2 cups desiccated coconut	
1 level tsp bicarbonate of soda	

1. Preheat the oven to 180 °C. Grease a baking tray.
2. Heat the margarine or oil with the sugar or fructose in a pot until the sugar dissolves, stirring regularly.
3. In a separate bowl, mix the oats, flour and coconut (and any of the optional extras) with a fork.
4. When the sugar has dissolved and is bubbling, add the bicarbonate of soda to the pot (this will foam and thicken a bit).
5. Make a well in the middle of the dry ingredients and pour in the hot mixture. Mix well and sprinkle onto the greased baking tray. Bake on the top shelf of the oven for a maximum of 15 minutes; it burns easily, so keep watch. Remove from the oven and leave to cool.
6. Store in an airtight container. Serve with rice, soy or cow's milk or yoghurt, or pour over a cup of fruit juice, such as mango.

DF, EF; WF; alt NF | Makes 10–12 servings

Banana muffins

2 well-ripened bananas, mashed	2 tsp baking powder
¼ cup oil or dairy-free margarine	1¼ cups rice flour + 1¼ cup rye/oat flour or
1 tsp vanilla essence	2½ cups cake flour
1 cup water	¼ tsp salt
⅓ cup white sugar or ¼ cup fructose	ground cinnamon for sprinkling
½ tsp bicarbonate of soda	

1. Preheat the oven to 180 °C. Grease a muffin pan or small loaf tin.
2. Mix the bananas, oil or margarine, vanilla essence, water and sugar until smooth.
3. In a separate bowl, mix the bicarbonate of soda, baking powder, flour and salt, and add to the banana mixture. Stir well. Spoon into the greased muffin pan, sprinkle with cinnamon and bake for 25 minutes or in a small loaf tin for 35–40 minutes.

EF; DF; NF; alt WF | Makes 10–12

TIP: Using cupcake papers to line muffin pans saves time on greasing. They also make it easier to take the muffins away as a snack.

Tammi's tasty corn & rice muffins

Tammi's tasty corn & rice muffins

2 cups rice flour
2 cups polenta or yellow maize meal (If using ordinary white maize meal, add ½ tsp custard powder for colour.)
½ cup fructose or brown sugar
1 Tbsp baking powder
a pinch of salt
½ cup chopped fresh dates or seedless raisins

2 cups boiling water
½ cup sunflower oil
3 medium eggs or 3 tsp Orgran No Egg powder mixed with 3 Tbsp hot water
½ cup hot water mixed with 2 Tbsp rice milk powder or ½ cup soy milk
1 tsp vanilla essence
1 Tbsp fructose or sugar mixed with ½ tsp ground cinnamon

1. Preheat the oven to 180 °C. Grease a muffin pan or line with cupcake papers.
2. Put the rice flour, polenta or maize meal, fructose or sugar, baking powder and salt in a bowl. Whisk with a fork to mix.
3. Allow the dates or raisins to soak in the boiling water for a few minutes. Then add the oil, eggs or egg substitute, milk and vanilla essence. Whisk lightly.
4. Make a well in the centre of the flour mixture and pour in the date mixture. Stir until just blended. Spoon the mixture into the muffin pan. Sprinkle the tops with the cinnamon and sugar and bake for 30 minutes. These are delicious plain or served with jam, butter or cottage cheese.

GF; DF; NF; alt EF; alt SF | Makes 12 large muffins

TIP: For savoury muffins, leave out the dates, use only a ¼ cup fructose, and add 1 tsp herb and garlic salt and 1 cup grated cheese. Mix well and bake. These can be served with soup or salad as a main meal.

Yummy wheaty muffins

1 cup Nutty Wheat flour (wholewheat)
1 cup white bread flour
2 cups baking powder
½ cup fructose or brown sugar

½ cup sunflower/canola oil
½ cup soy milk
1 cup seedless raisins soaked in 1 cup boiling water

1. Preheat the oven to 180 °C. Grease a muffin pan well.
2. Combine all the dry ingredients in a bowl, make a well in the centre and add the liquids, including the raisins and their water. Mix until just blended.
3. Spoon the mixture into the well-greased muffin pan and bake for 30–40 minutes. Serve plain or with jam. For a different treat, substitute chocolate chips (do not soak!) for the raisins and 1 cup boiling water.

EF; DF; NF; alt SF | Makes 12

5-minute vegan pancakes

1 cup flour (whichever kind you prefer)
1 Tbsp sugar (I use organic cane sugar)
2 tsp baking powder

⅛ tsp salt
1 cup soy milk or any milk of your choice
2 Tbsp vegetable oil

1. Combine the dry ingredients in a bowl. Add the milk and oil and mix until smooth.
2. Place a pan on the stove over a medium heat. Spray with non-stick cooking spray and add a little oil (approx. 1 tsp). The pan should now be ready for your batter, so spoon one ladleful of the mixture into it. Carefully flip the pancake when you see bubbles in the middle or if the edges are looking stiffened. Repeat until the batter is gone, and try not to eat them all while you're cooking them!
3. Serve with syrup and berries or sliced fruit.

EF; NF; alt DF | Makes 6–8

Wheat-free rye pizza dough

1 cup lukewarm water
1 Tbsp sugar
1 x 10 g sachet instant dry yeast

1 tsp salt
¼ cup extra-virgin olive oil
1 x 500 g pkt rye flour (stoneground or fine)

1. Mix the lukewarm water and sugar in a large flat-bottomed bowl and sprinkle over the yeast. Leave for 5 minutes to prove.
2. Add the salt and oil, then add the flour, 1 cup at a time, and stir with a large spoon. The dough will become stiff. When this happens, dust your hands with flour and lightly knead the dough. Rye flour has less elasticity than regular wheat flour, so gathering the dough and pushing down on it will suffice. If the dough is very stiff, drizzle over an extra 1–2 Tbsp oil and knead again lightly.
3. Leave the dough to rise for at least 30 minutes, more if the weather is cold.
4. Heat the oven to 180 °C. When it is hot, place two baking trays in the oven to heat.
5. When the dough has risen (it will rise to about 1.5 times its size), dust your hands with flour and punch it down. Halve the dough and place one half onto a sheet of baking paper the size of your baking trays. Pushing down with the heel of your hand, flatten the dough, working round and round until it is a largish rectangular shape. (You can use a rolling pin dusted with flour or maize meal to roll it flatter). Do the same with the other half of the dough. When both bases are flattened, place the baking paper onto the warmed baking trays. Spread with a tomato base and bake for about 7 minutes. Remove from the oven, add toppings of your choice (see opposite) and bake for a further 10 minutes, or until the bases are nicely browned and crisp.

WF; DF; EF; NF | Makes 2 bases

Brie & mushroom breakfast pizza

Pizza dough
about 2 cups lukewarm water
2 Tbsp sugar
1 x 10 g sachet instant dry yeast
1 Tbsp Ina Paarman's Seasoned Sea Salt
2 Tbsp olive oil
1 kg (about 6½ cups) bread flour

Topping per base
½ cup (1 x 125 ml pkt) Ina Paarman's
   Sundried Tomato Pesto
1 Tbsp oil
1 Tbsp butter
250 g mushrooms, sliced
Ina Paarman's Garlic Pepper Seasoning
   to taste
125 g Brie or Camembert cheese
4 eggs

1. Mix the lukewarm water and sugar in a large flat-bottomed bowl and sprinkle over the yeast. Leave for 5 minutes to prove.
2. Add the salt and oil, then add the flour, 1 cup at a time, and stir with a large spoon. The dough will become stiff and sticky. When this happens, dust your hands with flour and knead the dough by gathering it toward you with your palms and pushing it away again. If the dough is very stiff, drizzle over an extra 1–2 Tbsp oil and knead again lightly.
3. Leave the dough to rise for at least 30 minutes, more if the weather is cold.
4. Heat the oven to 200 °C. When hot, place two baking trays in it to heat.
5. When the dough has risen (it will rise to double its size), dust your hands with flour and punch it down. Divide the dough into four portions.
6. Roll out each portion of dough on a sheet of well-floured baking paper about 30 cm long. You should get two bases per sheet. Roll each base out very thinly to a rough rectangular shape. When all four bases are flattened, place the baking paper onto the warmed baking trays.
7. Spread the sundried tomato pesto over the bases, right to the edges, and bake for about 7 minutes.
8. Heat the oil and butter in a medium-sized frying pan and stir-fry the mushrooms over a high heat until beginning to soften. Season generously with garlic pepper seasoning.
9. Remove the half-baked pizza bases from the oven. Sprinkle over the cooked mushrooms and dot with small pieces of cheese. Make a hollow in the mushroom topping of each and break an egg into it.
10. Bake for a further 10 minutes until the bases are nicely browned and crisp. Cut into wedges and serve.

NF; alt DF; alt EF | Makes 4 pizzas

TIP: For a wheat-free version, use the dough recipe on page 20, using the same toppings, or play around and add your own. For a dairy-free version, simply leave out the cheese.

Tofu salad (page 25)

We don't need a melting pot in this country, folks. We need a salad bowl. In a salad bowl, you put in the different things. You want the vegetables – the lettuce, the cucumbers, the onions, the green peppers – to maintain their identity. You appreciate differences.

Jane Elliot

Salads, dressings and dips

A salad can contain any of a wide variety of foods: vegetables, fruit, pasta, legumes, eggs, grains, meat, poultry and seafood. It can include a mixture of cold and hot, raw and cooked ingredients. It can be simple (see the tomato and basil salad on page 25) or intricate (see the brown rice and lentil salad on page 29). Enhanced with a simple dressing or sauce, or enjoyed plain and crunchy with a dip such as hummus (see page 39), a salad can stand boldly on its own as a starter or even as a main meal.

We make use of fresh herbs, throwing together fresh-picked basil, chives or fennel with whatever fresh veggies are available. We also use spices; they have the power to create subtle or powerful new flavours.

Whether summer or winter, salads add fibre, taste, texture and colour to any meal.

Waldorf salad

Children love this salad. It makes a nutritious light meal or afternoon snack.

2 red apples, cored and diced
2 Granny Smith or Golden Delicious apples,
    cored and diced
3 bananas, sliced and sprinkled with
    lemon juice
1 cup chopped table celery, stalks only (save
    leaves for garnish)
1 small pineapple, peeled and diced

2 Tbsp roughly chopped pecan nuts or
    seedless raisins (optional)
1 cup tangy or egg-free mayonnaise or
    plain yoghurt
1 tsp curry powder
1 tsp sugar or xylitol or ½ tsp fructose powder
a pinch of salt or herb salt
mixed lettuce leaves to serve

1. Combine all of the ingredients and serve on a bed of lettuce or in a salad bowl.
2. Garnish with the celery leaves and serve.

WF; GF; alt SF; alt EF; alt NF | Serves 8

TIP: Add a can of tuna or some leftover diced chicken to make a balanced main course.

Three bean salad

I use frozen green beans in this salad as that way I always have a stand-by in case of unexpected guests. The warm dressing defrosts the beans and marinates them too. This is especially good with a braai.

1 x 1 kg pkt frozen cut green beans
2 x 410 g cans butter beans, drained
2 x 410 g cans baked beans in tomato sauce
1 onion, peeled and finely chopped
1 green pepper, deseeded and finely
    chopped (optional)

Dressing
1 cup vinegar
½ cup oil
½ cup seedless raisins
½ cup brown sugar or fructose powder

1. Combine all of the salad ingredients in a bowl.
2. Bring the salad dressing to the boil in a saucepan on the stove and simmer for 5 minutes, stirring until the sugar has dissolved. If using fructose, remove from the heat before adding the fructose.
3. Pour the hot dressing over the salad and cool before serving.

DF; WF; EF; GF; NF | Serves 10–12 as a side dish

TIP: Before adding the baked beans, I always keep some of the salad mix aside for my son, Lennie, who is allergic to tomato sauce.

Tomato & basil salad

This salad, with its bright colour contrasts, is very striking and is always popular at my table. Plus, it's so easy, you cannot believe!

1–2 large punnets baby roma or salad tomatoes, sliced in half lengthways
1 bunch fresh basil, washed and dried
1 x 200 g pkt Calamata olives
freshly ground black pepper to taste
1 clove garlic, crushed (optional)
olive oil for drizzling

1. Place the sliced tomatoes onto a salad platter. Tear the basil leaves and sprinkle over the tomatoes and place the olives in the spaces between.
2. Grind over some pepper, sprinkle with the garlic (if using) and top it all with a drizzle of olive oil. Serve with fresh bread or crackers.

WF; NF; EF; SF; GF; DF | Serves 6

TIP: Alternatively, use fresh baby spinach leaves instead of basil. For a more substantial salad, break up a wheel or two of feta cheese and sprinkle over.

Tofu salad

Thanks to my vegetarian friend, Caryn, who declares this salad a balanced meal.

1 cup couscous (wheat) or quinoa
2 English cucumbers, chopped
350 g baby tomatoes
10 black olives and 10 green olives
1 green or yellow pepper, deseeded and chopped
250 g smoked tofu, cubed into small pieces
1 onion, peeled and sliced into rings
1 red onion, peeled and sliced into rings

Dressing
½ cup olive oil
¼ cup red wine vinegar
1 Tbsp sugar
½ tsp dried origanum
½ tsp ground black pepper
½ tsp salt
1 clove garlic, crushed

1. Cook the couscous or quinoa according to the packet instructions. Place the remaining salad ingredients into a bowl.
2. Place the dressing ingredients in a jar and shake well. Chill before serving.
3. Pour the chilled dressing over the salad.
4. Just before serving, sprinkle over the cooked couscous or quinoa.

DF; EF; NF; alt GF; alt WF | Serves 8

Sam's green crunchy salad

My youngest son, Sam, loves celery, cucumber and apples. He asked me to chop up a 'salad' for him one day and this combo was born... It's great in winter served with hot foods for a hint of 'spring freshness'.

2 English cucumbers, chopped
6 Golden Delicious apples, cored and diced
1 bunch celery stalks (save a few leaves for garnish), chopped
1 Tbsp olive oil
½ cup apple juice
1 cup egg-free or tangy mayonnaise

½ tsp cumin
½ tsp ground cinnamon
½ tsp ground ginger
½ tsp turmeric
1 tsp medium curry powder (optional)
a pinch of salt
toasted sunflower seeds or almond flakes

1. In a glass bowl, layer the chopped cucumber, apple and celery, alternating layers.
2. Put the oil, apple juice, mayonnaise and spices in a bowl and whisk until blended. Pour this over the salad and chill in the fridge for a couple of hours.
3. Toss the salad before serving and garnish with celery leaves and a handful of toasted sunflower seeds or almond flakes.

WF; GF; DF; alt EF; alt NF | Serves 6–8 as a starter or side dish

Caramelised pear & blue cheese salad

1 Tbsp olive oil
1 x 410 g can sliced pears, drained
1 x 100 g pkt mixed lettuce leaves, washed and dried
1 x 80 g pkt rocket leaves, washed and dried
1 x 100 g wedge blue cheese, crumbled

1 small peanut brittle bar, crumbled or a handful of almonds (optional)
olive oil, balsamic vinegar and freshly ground black pepper to taste
10 baby potatoes, halved (optional, for a more substantial meal)

1. Heat the oil in a non-stick frying pan over a low to medium heat, add the canned pear slices and cook until they start to caramelise. Remove the pears and allow to cool.
2. Place the lettuce leaves on a platter, sprinkle over the rocket leaves and layer the rest of the ingredients, finishing with the blue cheese and peanut brittle (if using). Drizzle over some olive oil and balsamic vinegar, and grind over some black pepper.
3. If using, season the baby potatoes and drizzle with olive oil, then roast in the oven until soft. Add to the salad and serve.

WF; EF; GF; alt NF | Serves 6

Caramelised pear
& blue cheese salad

Sushi rice salad

I love sushi and do enjoy making it, but find all the rolling and assembly really time consuming. This has all the makings of sushi, but thrown together in salad form – now that's something I can handle! It's very easy and sure to satisfy those sushi cravings. It makes a delicious and very impressive starter or even a main course for a dinner party.

Sushi rice
3 cups uncooked sushi rice
3 cups water
½ cup Japanese rice vinegar (sometimes I cheat and use apple cider vinegar instead)
½ cup sugar
1 tsp salt
1 Tbsp sesame seeds

Salad
1 large ripe avocado
1 red onion, peeled and finely sliced
1 large English cucumber, quartered lengthways, deseeded and chopped into sticks
2 carrots, peeled and julienned
1 x 100 g pkt smoked salmon offcuts (optional)
2 sheets nori (paper-thin sheets of dried seaweed), cut into thin 5 cm-long strips with scissors

1. Rinse the rice thoroughly in a sieve and drain well. Bring the water to the boil in a medium saucepan and add the rice. Cover, reduce the heat and simmer for 20 minutes or until the liquid is absorbed.
2. In a small saucepan, bring the vinegar to the boil with the sugar and salt, stirring until the sugar is dissolved. Remove from the heat.
3. In a small, dry pan, toast the sesame seeds over a moderate heat, stirring, until golden and fragrant. Transfer to a small bowl.
4. Once the rice is cooked, uncover and cool to room temperature. Place the rice in a large flat bowl (I use a large glass casserole dish). Evenly sprinkle the vinegar mix over the rice and, using a spatula, mix the rice and vinegar by cutting through the rice with the blade of the spatula. Try to avoid using metal, as it will change the flavour of the rice. Be careful not to break the kernels of the rice or to flatten it, as it won't have the same look and feel to it. Once well mixed, use a fan or plate to fan the rice down to room temperature. By doing this, the rice will have the right glossy look while still being nice and sticky.
5. Rinse a deep, medium-sized, round bowl with cold water; do not dry. Transfer the rice to this bowl and pat down into the mould. Turn the rice out onto a platter.
6. Peel, pit and quarter the avocado, then cut crosswise into thin slices. Arrange the avocado, onion, cucumber, carrot and smoked salmon (if using) around the rice. Sprinkle over the toasted sesame seeds and nori strips. Drizzle over a dressing of your choice (see pages 36–37).

WF; DF; GF; EF | Serves 4–6 as a main or 8–10 as a starter

TIP: *Tezu* is important when preparing sushi. Many people don't like the stickiness of the rice on their hands so they spread the rice with a wooden spoon. However, the best way to handle sushi rice is with your hands and the best way to keep it from sticking to your hands is to use tezu. Tezu is simply a mix of one part water and one part rice vinegar. Apply it to your hands sparingly and you'll be able to handle rice without it sticking. Also soak some into a clean kitchen cloth and use this to clean your knife after every few slices when cutting rolled sushi.

Apple & cucumber rice salad

With the addition of a can of tuna or a leftover sliced chicken breast, this salad becomes a meal!

3 Golden Delicious apples, cored and diced
1 whole cucumber, quartered down the length, then sliced
1 bunch seedless green grapes, halved
3 cups cooked brown rice

1 cup egg-free or tangy mayonnaise
½ cup plain Bulgarian yoghurt (optional)
1 tsp dill
herb salt and black pepper to taste

1. Combine all of the ingredients in a glass bowl and garnish with a few extra grapes before serving.

GF; SF; WF; NF; alt DF; alt EF | Serves 6

Brown rice & lentil salad

This healthy salad is my all-time favourite. It's both tasty and full of fibre. Omit ingredients according to allergies. The salad keeps well for days and is a good school or work lunch addition.

1¼ cups brown rice
1 cup brown lentils
½ cup seedless raisins
½ cup sunflower seeds
¾ cup dried apricots, roughly chopped
1 cup coarsely grated carrot
1 cup chopped celery stalks and leaves
1 green or red pepper, deseeded and diced
1 medium onion, peeled and diced
½ cup chopped parsley (optional)

Dressing
¾ cup sunflower oil
½ cup apple cider vinegar or ¾ cup lemon juice
1 Tbsp curry powder
½ tsp cumin
½ tsp ground ginger
2 Tbsp honey
1 tsp soy sauce

1. Cook the rice and lentils in separate pots according to the packet instructions. Mix the hot rice and lentils with the raisins, sunflower seeds and apricots.
2. Combine all of the dressing ingredients and add to the warm rice mixture. Allow to cool.
3. Add the remaining ingredients and leave to stand for several hours before serving.

WF; DF; EF; NF; GF | Serves 4 as a main or 6 as a side dish

Salad sandwich

Salad sandwich

This makes an amazing lunch for hungry youngsters.

a few slices of freshly baked rye bread (see
page 106) or bread of your choice
a handful of frilly lettuce leaves
a handful of chopped mixed raw nuts
(walnuts, pecans, cashews, almonds, etc.)
a handful of seed mix (flax, sesame,
sunflower, pumpkin, etc.)
extra-virgin cold-pressed olive oil
for drizzling
juice of 1 freshly squeezed lemon

Finely chop your choice of the following:
tomato, celery, cucumber, red onion, sweet
pepper, carrot and apple

Mix together:
1 clove garlic, crushed
1 chilli, deseeded and chopped (optional)
1 tsp chopped parsley
1 tsp torn basil leaves
1 tsp chopped coriander leaves
1 small spring onion, chopped
2–3 dried dates, pitted and chopped
Herbamare® Organic Herb Seasoning Salt
and freshly ground pepper to taste
a few sprigs of fresh dill or fennel

1. Cover the slices of bread with washed and dried lettuce leaves.
2. Arrange the chopped ingredients on the lettuce.
3. Top this with the garlic mixture.
4. Sprinkle over the chopped nuts and seeds.
5. Drizzle with the olive oil and lemon juice and serve immediately.

SF; DF; alt GF; alt WF | Serves 1 or more

Easy bean salad

This salad is quick and easy, and tasty too! It's delicious with a braai.

2 x 410 g cans baked beans
1 onion, peeled and finely chopped
3 pickled cucumbers, diced

1 Tbsp chutney
¼ cup egg-free or tangy mayonnaise

1. Mix all the ingredients in a bowl, chill for an hour or overnight and serve.

WF; GF; DF; alt EF | Serves 6

Curried broccoli salad

1–2 heads of broccoli
½ tsp cumin
½ tsp turmeric
½ tsp ground ginger

¼ tsp ground cinnamon
1 cup egg-free or tangy mayonnaise
toasted flaked almonds to serve (optional)

1. Break the broccoli into florets, soak, rinse and steam – set aside to cool.
2. Mix the spices with 1 tsp hot water and add to the mayonnaise.
3. Place the broccoli in a bowl and pour over the curry mayonnaise. Chill for a few hours before serving, garnished with flaked almonds if desired. Make double as it is delicious!

WF; DF; GF; alt EF | Serves 6–8

Sweet potato salad

This is such a pretty salad and the beta-carotene practically screams at you! It travels well and is a great alternative to the starchier white potatoes. Flavoured with toasted pecans, chewy, tangy cranberries and lemon, it's perfect with roast lamb or grilled chicken. Fancy or plain, it's good no matter what meal you serve it with.

2 large yellow sweet potatoes, peeled and
   diced into 2.5 cm cubes
2 large orange sweet potatoes or 4 carrots,
   peeled and diced
olive oil for drizzling
1 tsp chopped fresh rosemary or ½ tsp dried
salt and freshly ground black pepper to taste
1 Tbsp chopped fresh parsley
½–1 red onion, peeled and finely diced

¼ cup dried cranberries
¼ cup toasted and chopped pecan nuts

Dressing
2 Tbsp olive oil
2 Tbsp fresh lemon juice
2 Tbsp honey
1–2 Tbsp soy sauce or to taste
freshly ground black pepper to taste

1. Preheat the oven to 180 °C. Place the diced sweet potatoes (and carrots) in a shallow baking dish. Drizzle with olive oil and sprinkle with the rosemary, salt and pepper. Stir to coat. Roast for 25–30 minutes or until just tender. Allow to cool slightly.
2. In a small bowl, whisk together the dressing ingredients.
3. Transfer the potatoes to a medium serving bowl and sprinkle over the parsley, onion and cranberries.
4. Drizzle with the dressing and sprinkle over the pecans just before serving, so that they remain crunchy. Serve either warm, cold or at room temperature.

DF; WF; GF; EF; YF | Serves 6

Curried broccoli salad

Chunky potato
pesto salad

Mandarin & avocado salad

½ cup flaked almonds
1 red-leaf lettuce
1 red onion, peeled and sliced into rings
2 x 310 g cans mandarin orange
   segments, drained
2 avocados, peeled, pitted and sliced

Dressing
¼ cup oil
¼ cup apple cider vinegar
2 Tbsp sugar
1 Tbsp lemon juice
½ tsp salt
½ tsp mustard powder
½ tsp finely grated onion (optional)
¼ tsp Tabasco (optional)

1. Dry roast the almonds in a pan over a medium heat until just beginning to brown, shaking the pan regularly to prevent burning.
2. Combine all of the dressing ingredients in a jar and shake well.
3. Arrange the lettuce, onion, mandarin segments and avocado on a platter. Drizzle over the dressing and sprinkle with the toasted almonds.

EF; WF; DF; GF | Serves 6

Chunky potato pesto salad

8 potatoes or 1 kg baby potatoes
olive oil for drizzling
½ tsp sea salt flakes
freshly ground black pepper to taste

Pesto
1 bunch of fresh basil, washed and dried
2–3 large cloves garlic, crushed or
   1 heaped tsp crushed garlic
1 cup sunflower seeds, dry roasted
¼ cup olive oil

1. Boil the potatoes until tender, but not mushy. Drain and leave to cool. Then cut each potato into large chunks, leaving the skins on. Place the potatoes in a wide, shallow bowl, pour over a little olive oil and season with salt and pepper.
2. Cut up the basil with scissors and mix with the garlic, sunflower seeds and olive oil. Leave to stand for an hour to allow the flavours to develop and combine. Pesto will keep in a jar in the fridge for up to a week – pour a little extra olive oil over the top to seal before closing the lid.
3. Spoon the pesto over the potatoes and serve cold or at room temperature.

WF; DF; NF; EF; SF | Serves 4

Hummus dressing

½ cup tangy or egg-free mayonnaise
2 Tbsp hummus
½ cup water
2 Tbsp balsamic vinegar

2 tsp sugar
½ tsp crushed garlic
a pinch of salt
freshly ground black pepper to taste

1. Place all of the ingredients in a small jar and shake well.

WF; DF; GF; alt EF

Ginger & soy dressing

½ tsp crushed garlic
1 tsp crushed fresh ginger or ½ tsp powdered
1 Tbsp soy sauce or tamari (wheat-free soy sauce)

½ cup balsamic vinegar
½ cup brown sugar
1 cup olive oil or ½ cup olive oil blended with ½ cup sunflower oil

1. Place all of the ingredients in a jar and shake well before pouring over a salad.
2. I particularly enjoy this dressing with a salad of sliced pears, rocket and goat's cheese.

EF; DF; alt WF; alt GF

Simple & easy soy dressing

¼ cup rice or apple cider vinegar
2 Tbsp soy sauce or tamari (wheat-free soy sauce)
2 Tbsp sugar

½ cup olive oil
2 Tbsp water
1 Tbsp honey

1. Pour all of the ingredients directly into a salad dressing bottle or any empty, clean jar. Shake well and drizzle over salad.
2. The dressing keeps well in the fridge and is delicious over any green salad.

DF; EF; alt WF; alt GF

Ginger salad dressing

½ cup rice vinegar
1 Tbsp vegetable oil
1 Tbsp soy sauce or tamari (wheat-free soy sauce)

1 tsp peeled and grated fresh ginger
1 clove garlic, minced
¼–¾ tsp prepared wasabi (optional)

1. Place all of the ingredients in a small bowl and whisk before drizzling over a salad.

DF; EF; alt WF; alt GF

Japanese salad dressing

½ cup minced onion
½ cup peanut oil
⅓ cup rice wine vinegar
2 Tbsp water
2 Tbsp minced fresh ginger root
2 Tbsp minced celery
2 Tbsp tomato sauce

4 tsp soy sauce or tamari (wheat-free soy sauce)
2 tsp white sugar
2 tsp lemon juice
½ tsp minced garlic
½ tsp salt
¼ tsp ground black pepper

1. Place all of the ingredients in a medium-sized bowl and whisk. Pour over salad and enjoy.
2. This recipe makes enough for two salads; the extra keeps well in the fridge.

DF; EF; alt GF; alt WF

Onion salad dressing

3 Tbsp rice wine vinegar
4 Tbsp vegetable oil
½ tsp sugar

1 tsp soy sauce or tamari (wheat-free soy sauce)
1 Tbsp grated onion

1. Place all of the ingredients in a medium-sized bowl and whisk.
2. Make this dressing the day before and chill in the fridge. Stir just before using to reblend the ingredients.

DF; EF; alt WF; alt GF

Lentil pâté

Lentils are a cheap, easy-to-store source of fibre and protein. They often contain small stones or twigs so must be checked before cooking. This pâté is tastier with eggs, but these can be omitted for those with an egg allergy.

3 cups water
1½ cups dried lentils, rinsed
3 Tbsp olive oil
2 large onions, peeled and finely chopped

2 hard-boiled eggs (optional)
¼ cup walnuts
salt and freshly ground black pepper to taste
2 Tbsp chopped fresh parsley

1. Bring the water to the boil, add the cleaned lentils and lower the heat. Do not add salt as it toughens the lentils and they will take longer to cook. Cover and simmer for 40–50 minutes or until the lentils are very soft. Drain and set aside.
2. Heat the oil in medium-sized frying pan and sauté the onions over a medium heat for about 15 minutes until caramelised. Do not stir too much or the onions will not caramelise.
3. Stir in the drained lentils, remove from the heat and allow to cool.
4. If using, shell the eggs and cut in quarters. Put the eggs, lentil mixture and walnuts into a food processor and blend until smooth. Season with salt and pepper.
5. Mound on a platter and sprinkle with the parsley. Serve as a spread on toast or crackers or with crudités.

WF; DF; GF; alt EF | Serves 8–10 as an appetizer

Hummus

Hummus is one of the more popular Mediterranean dips. Served with fresh or toasted pita bread, hummus makes for a great snack or appetizer. Tahini (sesame seed paste) is an important part of the hummus recipe and cannot be substituted. However, it can be omitted.

2 x 400 g cans chickpeas, drained and liquid reserved
2 Tbsp olive oil + 1–2 Tbsp extra for later
¼ cup tahini
2 cloves garlic, crushed

3–5 Tbsp lemon juice (depending on taste)
½ tsp salt
¼ cup liquid from chickpeas or water
¼ tsp paprika or 1 tsp chopped fresh parsley (whichever you prefer)

1. Place the chickpeas, 2 Tbsp oil, tahini, garlic, lemon juice and salt in a blender or food processor.
2. Add ¼ cup of the chickpea liquid (or water) and blend for 3–5 minutes on low until thoroughly mixed and smooth.
3. Place in a serving bowl and, using the back of a spoon, create a shallow well in the centre of the hummus. Add a small amount (1–2 Tbsp) of olive oil to the well. Garnish with paprika or parsley (whichever you prefer) and serve immediately with cut-up raw vegetables, chips or fresh, warm or toasted pita bread.
4. This dip keeps well in the fridge and freezes well too.

WF; NF; DF; GF; SF | Serves 12 as a starter (makes about 2 cups)

TIPS: For a spicier hummus, add a sliced red chilli or a dash of cayenne pepper before blending. In the Middle East, hummus is traditionally sprinkled with a delicious mix called za'atar – a combination of origanum, basil and thyme, blended with salt and sesame seeds. If you can get hold of some, try it – it has a delicate, subtle flavour that enhances the hummus.

What garlic is to salad, insanity is to art.

Augustus Saint-Gaudens

Broccoli soup (page 44)

Soup is a lot like a family. Each ingredient enhances the others;
each batch has its own characteristics; and it needs
time to simmer to reach full flavour.

Marge Kennedy

Soups

Whether the starter course of a special dinner or the last resort of tired parents, a sparse pantry and hungry children, soup can be made delicious with just a little inspiration.

And there's nothing better when you're ill than a steaming bowl of chicken soup. So many programmes try to unify people of different origins, but what many of us have learnt is that the unifying factor among all people is Mom's chicken soup … or Tammi's chicken soup. Find it on page 49. Replete with garlic and ginger, and full of chicken and veggies, it is a panacea for mind, body and soul!

Anya's Seattle fruit & yoghurt soup

I met my French friend Anya, a gourmet chef and psychologist, when I moved to Seattle in 2001. She taught me the art of cooking simply and celebrating a few tasty ingredients. Her table is a palette of bright colours made up of fresh fruits and vegetables. This simple soup can be made up to 48 hours ahead of time and is served chilled. It's perfect for a hot summer's day.

4 cups plain or vanilla low-fat yoghurt
1 tsp vanilla extract (if using plain yoghurt)
6 cups orange juice or any other fruit juice
   (mango, apple, berry, etc.)

2 Tbsp lemon juice or to taste
organic cane sugar, stevia or honey to taste
fresh or frozen berries or fresh fruit to serve
ground cinnamon to serve

1. Whisk all of the ingredients, except the fruit and cinnamon, in a large bowl and adjust taste according to preference. The soup should not be as sweet as yoghurt dessert, but have some sweetness to it, especially if the berries are very sour.
2. Serve this with either fresh or frozen berries (defrosting in the fridge overnight works well), fresh mango or any other fresh fruit.
3. Spoon the yoghurt mix into soup bowls and add a heaped tablespoon of berries or fruit to each bowl. Top with ground cinnamon just before serving.

WF; GF; EF; NF | Serves 8

Cold melon soup

1 cup orange juice
3 Tbsp lime juice
2 Tbsp honey
4 cups peeled, deseeded and chopped
   cantaloupe (spanspek)

4 cups peeled, deseeded and chopped
   honeydew melon
2 cups Appletizer™ or sparkling wine
nasturtium flowers or mint leaves to garnish
sour cream to serve (optional)

1. Purée the orange juice, lime juice, honey, half of the cantaloupe and half of the honeydew melon in a food processor or blender. Transfer to a large bowl.
2. Finely chop or grate the remaining cantaloupe and melon and stir into the purée. Then stir in the Appletizer™ or sparkling wine. Refrigerate until ready to serve.
3. Serve chilled in bowls with a nasturtium flower or sprig of mint floating in each. If you would like to, add a tablespoon of sour cream to each bowl before serving.

WF; DF; EF; GF; NF | Serves 2–4

Cold tomato & cucumber soup

My mom, Joan, has been making this delicious soup since my childhood. It is very quick and easy to make, but allow time to chill before serving.

2 x 500 g cartons buttermilk
 (reserve ½ cup for decoration)
1 x 400 g can tomato soup

1 large English cucumber, grated
 (reserve some for decoration)

1. Mix the buttermilk, tomato soup and grated cucumber in a bowl. Cover and chill for a few hours, preferably overnight.
2. Serve in soup bowls or tea cups, with a dollop of the reserved buttermilk and a little grated cucumber sprinkled over for decoration.

WF; GF; EF; NF | Serves 4–6

TIP: This soup can be made using goat's milk yoghurt instead of buttermilk.

Broccoli soup

The fresh, green colour and full flavour gives this soup real appetite appeal, and it's seriously good for you!

3 Tbsp Ina Paarman's Vegetable Stock Powder
5 cups water
3 medium potatoes, peeled and cut into
 small cubes
2 onions, peeled and finely chopped

4 cloves garlic, crushed
2 tsp Ina Paarman's Seasoned Sea Salt
500 g broccoli, cut into florets
1 bunch of chives, finely snipped
1–2 wheels feta cheese, crumbled (optional)

1. In a large pot, dissolve the stock powder in the water and add the potatoes, onions, garlic and salt. Cook for 10 minutes over a medium heat. Add the broccoli florets and bring to the boil for 8–10 minutes, until the broccoli is just tender.
2. Liquidise in a food processor, taste for seasoning and add half the chives.
3. To serve, reheat and garnish with the remaining chives and the feta cheese (if using). Alternatively, in summer, serve cold, topped with the feta cheese and chives.

WF; GF; EF; NF; alt DF | Serves 4

TIP: This recipe doubles and triples easily and deliciously!

Green pea soup

This quick and easy soup makes a delicious winter meal or starter.

3 Tbsp olive or sunflower oil
2 onions, peeled and chopped
2 celery stalks including leaves, chopped
1 clove garlic, crushed

3 carrots, peeled and cut into chunks
5–6 cups vegetable or chicken stock
1 x 500 g pkt split peas, rinsed (not soaked)
salt and ground black pepper to taste

1. Heat the oil in a pot over a low heat and sauté the onions until soft and flavourful. Add the celery and garlic, and sauté for a further 2 minutes. Add the carrots and stir to coat.
2. Add the stock and peas, then turn up the heat and bring to the boil. Reduce the heat and simmer for 25–30 minutes, stirring regularly. Add salt and pepper to taste.
3. Allow to cool a little and then liquidise with a stick blender or push through a sieve. This soup keeps well in the fridge for 2–3 days and can be reheated as needed. Serve with rye toast, rice cakes or fresh rolls for a delicious meal.

EF; DF; NF; WF; GF | Serves 6

Joey's beef & barley soup

Delicious, nutritious and easy, this meal-in-a-pot soup was created by my eldest son, Joey, from a combination of a few recipes. We eat it often in winter.

2 large onions, peeled and diced
½ bunch of table celery, chopped
little oil for frying
500 g lean beef mince
1 x 500 g pkt frozen mixed vegetables (peas, corn, green beans and carrots)
1–2 cloves garlic

1 tsp ground ginger
1 tsp cumin
3–4 bay leaves
½–1 cup pearl barley (use millet if gluten intolerant)
6–8 cups vegetable or chicken stock
salt and ground black pepper to taste

1. In a large soup pot, sauté the onions and celery over a low heat in a little oil until glassy.
2. Turn the heat to medium and add the beef mince to brown. Add the frozen vegetables, garlic and spices, put on the lid and allow to defrost for 5–10 minutes, stirring intermittently.
3. In the meanwhile, rinse the barley thoroughly. Add the barley and stock to the pot, close the lid and simmer for 45–60 minutes. Season to taste. Remove the bay leaves before serving.
4. This soup can be made in a slow cooker. Simply add all the ingredients, close the lid and leave to cook on low for 8–10 hours.

EF; DF; NF; WF | Serves 6–8

Onion soup

4 Tbsp butter or olive oil (or a mix of both)
8 onions, peeled and thinly sliced
4 Tbsp wheat/rye/rice flour
6–8 cups boiling water
3 Tbsp Ina Paarman's Vegetable Stock
   Powder or Pareve Chicken Stock Powder
4 bay leaves

freshly ground black pepper to taste
1 French loaf, sliced
olive oil for brushing
grated Cheddar or Parmesan
   cheese (optional)
chopped fresh parsley to garnish

1. Heat the butter or oil in a pot over a medium heat and sauté the onions until glassy. Increase the temperature and allow the onions to start browning. Remove from the heat, sprinkle the flour over the onions and stir well.
2. Pour over the boiling water and add the stock powder, bay leaves and pepper to taste. Put back on the heat, bring to the boil and then simmer for 30 minutes with the lid on.
3. Lightly brush the slices of bread with olive oil and toast lightly on both sides under the grill. Sprinkle over the cheese (if using) and place under the grill again for a few seconds to melt. Sprinkle the slices with parsley and float the toasts on top of the onion soup to serve.

EF; NF; alt WF; alt GF; alt DF | Serves 4–6

Asian beef & noodle soup

This soup is light, but filling and has an interesting combination of flavours. Substitute cooked chicken for the beef.

250 g minute/tenderised steak, thinly sliced
   into strips
6 cups vegetable or chicken stock
2 Tbsp soy sauce or tamari (wheat-free
   soy sauce)
2 Tbsp chilli sauce or regular tomato sauce
1 Tbsp ground ginger
1 Tbsp crushed garlic

a pinch of cayenne pepper
2½ cups thinly sliced red or green cabbage
3 carrots, peeled and sliced into strips
1 cup sliced button mushrooms
½ cup frozen corn kernels
4 spring onions, thinly sliced
2 tsp sesame oil (optional)
1 x 250 g pkt rice noodles, broken up

1. Stir-fry the beef strips in a little oil over a high heat. Remove from the pan and set aside.
2. Mix the stock, soy sauce, chilli sauce, ginger, garlic and pepper in a large pot. Bring to a simmer.
3. Add the cabbage and carrots and cook for 5 minutes. Add the mushrooms and corn, and simmer for 3 minutes. Add the beef and spring onions, heat through and then stir in the sesame oil (if using).
4. A couple of minutes before serving, throw in the broken-up rice noodles and mix well.

DF; NF; EF; alt WF; alt GF | Serves 6

Asian beef & noodle soup

Butternut soup

This slightly sweet soup has a rich orange colour and a delicious aroma – it's my favourite! This soup improves with standing, so can be made a day or two in advance and reheated just before serving. I double this recipe and freeze half in individual portions for snacks.

3 Tbsp olive oil or butter
2 onions, peeled and chopped
6–8 cups peeled and cubed butternut
1 tsp medium curry powder
1 tsp ground ginger
½ tsp ground cinnamon

1–2 green apples, unpeeled, cored
   and chopped
4 cups vegetable stock or water
1½ cups rice/cow's milk
½ cup apple juice (optional)
salt and ground black pepper to taste

1. Heat the oil or butter in a large pot and sauté the onions until soft (do not brown). Add the butternut and sauté for about 3 minutes to develop the flavours. Add the curry powder, ginger and cinnamon, blending with the vegetables.
2. Add the apples, stock or water, milk and juice (if using). Simmer for 20–25 minutes until the vegetables are tender. Liquidise with a stick blender and season to taste.

EF; NF; WF; GF; alt DF | Serves 6–8

Lentil soup

2 onions, peeled and diced
2 celery stalks, chopped
little oil for frying
1 tsp crushed garlic
1 tsp cumin
½ tsp ground ginger
1 x 500 g pkt brown lentils, rinsed (not soaked)

6 cups vegetable stock or water
4 carrots, peeled and roughly chopped
2 baby marrows/courgettes, sliced
1 x 410 g can chopped peeled tomatoes or
   4 potatoes, peeled and diced
½ tsp sugar (optional)
salt and ground black pepper to taste

1. In a pot, sauté the onions and celery in a little oil until glassy. Add the garlic, cumin and ginger and stir-fry.
2. Add the rinsed lentils and stock or water, and bring to the boil. Add the carrots, marrows and tomatoes or potatoes and cook for 45–60 minutes. Season to taste. If using canned tomatoes, add the sugar.
3. This soup freezes well, but do not add the potato if freezing as it will become mushy. Rather defrost the soup over a low heat, then add the potato and cook for an extra 30 minutes. It keeps well in the fridge for up to one week.

EF; DF; NF; WF; GF | Serves 6 as a main meal or 8 as a starter

Tammi's chicken soup

Chicken soup is often called the 'panacea for all ills'. This soup is more a stew than a traditional broth. It is a balanced meal in a pot.

2 large onions, peeled and diced
3–4 celery stalks, chopped
little olive or sunflower oil for frying
2 cups pearl barley, washed and soaked or
    1 cup quinoa* (if gluten is an issue)
2 cloves garlic, crushed
3 large carrots, peeled and cut into chunks

2–3 bay leaves
½ tsp powdered ginger
8–10 cups vegetable or chicken stock
1 whole chicken, preroasted in the oven (this
    can be done in advance and frozen, then
    added frozen to the soup pot)
salt and ground black pepper to taste

1. In a large soup pot, sauté the onions and celery in a little oil until soft and starting to brown.
2. Add the barley, garlic, carrots, bay leaves and ginger, and stir to combine.
3. Add the stock and chicken, put on the lid and bring to the boil. Turn down the heat to medium, remove the lid and simmer, stirring occasionally, for 1 hour.
4. After an hour, take the chicken out of the pot and remove the carcass bones. Return the chicken flesh to the pot and continue simmering for a further hour. Add extra water if necessary and season to taste.

*If using quinoa instead of barley, only add near the end of cooking and boil for a further 10 minutes.

EF; DF; NF; WF; alt GF | Serves 10–12

TIPS: For a more economical and thinner soup, substitute chicken necks and giblets for the whole chicken. This is a thick, nutritious soup and a great winter meal. For small babies, it can be puréed, but it's suitable as is from nine months.
For a more 'classic' chicken broth, use half or quarter the amount of chicken and substitute ½ cup dry noodles for the barley. Add the dry noodles to the pot when the soup is ready and cook for an extra 10 minutes.

As the days grow short, some faces grow long. But not mine. Every autumn, when the wind turns cold and darkness comes early, I am suddenly happy. It's time to start making soup again.

Leslie Newman

Minestrone

Minestrone

As this is a vegetarian soup, the true Italian name is '*minestra*', however, it's more easily recognised as 'minestrone'.

3 Tbsp olive oil
1 large onion, peeled and chopped
2 celery stalks with leaves, chopped
2 cloves garlic, crushed
1 leek, chopped
3 carrots, peeled and chopped
1 turnip, chopped
1 small piece cabbage, shredded
¼ cauliflower or broccoli head, cut up
1 large potato, peeled and cubed

½ cup chopped fresh parsley
8 cups vegetable stock
1 Tbsp tomato paste
½ tsp sugar
1 cup frozen peas
1 cup frozen green beans
1 x 410 g can butter beans, drained
½ cup uncooked fusilli or rice noodles
salt and freshly ground black pepper to taste

1. Heat the oil in a large pot and sauté the onion and celery.
2. Add the garlic and stir, then add the remaining fresh vegetables, the parsley, stock, tomato paste and sugar. Simmer for 45 minutes. Add the frozen vegetables, butter beans and noodles, and simmer for a further 15 minutes. Season to taste.

EF; DF; NF; alt WF; alt GF | Serves 8 as a main meal or 12 as a starter

Apple & celery soup

1 Tbsp butter
2 medium onions, peeled and chopped
1 bunch of fresh celery, washed and diced
2 large Granny Smith apples, unpeeled,
   cored and chopped

4 cups vegetable stock
1 Tbsp brown sugar
salt and ground black pepper to taste
½–1 cup rice/soy/cow's milk
chopped fresh parsley to serve

1. Heat the butter in a large saucepan and sauté the onions. Add the celery and continue to sauté on a low heat.
2. Add the apples and cook for a further 2 minutes, then add the stock, sugar, salt and pepper (beware of too much salt if using stock made from cubes). Bring to the boil, then reduce the heat and simmer, covered, for 15–20 minutes. Don't overcook or the celery flavour will become jaded and the colours dull.
3. Allow to cool a little before liquidising thoroughly. Pass through a large mesh sieve to ensure there are no stringy threads of celery remaining. Check for seasoning and consistency, adding a little milk to taste. Serve in warmed bowls, sprinkled with parsley.

EF; NF; WF; GF; alt DF | Serves 4–6

Rye pizza with tomato & basil (page 62)

Cooking is an art and patience a virtue ... Careful shopping, fresh ingredients and an unhurried approach are nearly all you need. There is one more thing – love. Love for food and love for those you invite to your table. With a combination of these things you can be an artist - not perhaps in the representational style of a Dutch master, but rather more like Gauguin, the naïve, or Van Gogh, the impressionist. Plates or pictures of sunshine taste of happiness and love.

Keith Floyd, *A Feast of Floyd*

Mains

The truth is, I love cooking. In the world in which we live, where days are measured in 15-minute increments and it's all about convenience, I almost hesitate to admit this. I enjoy the sensuality of the aromas and textures, the tasting and the creativity. I love to feed my hungry and appreciative audience – my family – a tangible expression of love straight from my 'Jewish mother' heart.

I read recipe books as a means of inspiration. I don't follow the steps. I shut the book and create, using whatever fresh ingredients are at hand. My herbs and spices are both a luxury and a necessity. An old friend once taught me how to blend spices from scratch and my sons keep a potted herb garden ready for the picking.

My eldest son, Joey, already an accomplished and capable cook and baker, also garners great pleasure from finding and adapting interesting recipes.

Baked fish

This is a low-glycaemic index fish dish.

2 onions, peeled and sliced
1 x 410 g can butter beans, drained
2 Tbsp olive oil
Ina Paarman's Garlic and Herb Salt to taste

1 kg whole yellowtail or Cape salmon,
 filleted with skin on
2 Tbsp uncooked rolled or breakfast oats
½ cup egg-free or tangy mayonnaise

1. Preheat the oven to 180 °C.
2. Place the onions and beans into a casserole dish, drizzle over the olive oil, season with the salt and bake in the oven for 15 minutes.
3. Remove from the oven and place the fish, skin-side down, on top of the onion-bean mix. Sprinkle over the oats and spoon the mayonnaise on top. Bake for 10 minutes, then switch on the grill and grill until lightly browned. Serve with basmati rice and a green salad.

DF; WF; NF; alt EF | Serves 4–6

Fish cakes

Mackerel is a good source of omega-3 fatty acid and calcium. I often double this recipe as the fish balls are good as snacks or in lunch boxes. They keep well in the fridge.

2 large sweet potatoes or 4 regular potatoes
2 x 425 g cans jack mackerel, drained and
 mashed (including bones)
2 large onions, peeled and chopped
1 large carrot, peeled and grated
herb salt to taste

2 tsp Orgran No Egg powder mixed with
 2 Tbsp hot water OR 2 eggs
rye/rice/wheat flour or maize meal
 for dusting
sunflower oil for cooking

1. Preheat the oven to 190 °C. Pour oil onto a baking tray, 0.5–1 cm deep.
2. Boil or microwave the potatoes until soft. Allow to cool, then remove their skins and mash.
3. Mix all of the ingredients, except the flour and oil, in a large bowl. If the mixture is very wet, add a little flour to firm it up.
4 With floured hands, pat tablespoonfuls of the mixture into balls and place them in the oil on the baking tray, leaving spaces in-between. Roast for about 1 hour until brown.
5. Serve with a green salad, some lemon wedges and bowls of tomato sauce or chutney for dipping.

DF; NF; SF; alt EF; alt WF; alt GF | Makes approx. 18

Fish cakes

Nothing would be more tiresome than eating and drinking if
God had not made them a pleasure as well as a necessity.

Voltaire

Wheat-free crustless quiche

This quiche can be served with fresh rye bread, soup or a salad. The 'filling' determines the flavour.

Filling options:
caramelised onion (onion sautéd in olive
    oil with a little brown sugar and a drop of
    vinegar), rosemary and baby tomatoes OR
smoked salmon strips, cracked black pepper
    and dill OR
sliced mushrooms, onion and red pepper
    with feta cubes and grated cheese OR
peppadews, sliced baby marrow and corn
    (frozen works great)

Quiche custard:
½ cup soy/cow's milk
6 extra-large eggs
1 tsp baking powder
salt and pepper to taste

1. Preheat the oven to 180 °C. Grease a quiche/pie dish.
2. Concoct a filling using the options above, or create your own. Spoon your filling into the greased dish.
3. Beat together the quiche custard ingredients and pour over the filling.
4. Bake for 45 minutes until the custard has set.

WF; GF; NF; alt DF | Serves 4

TIP: Make individual mini quiches: grease a muffin pan, place a spoonful of filling into each hole and then pour over the quiche custard, filling each to three-quarters full. Bake for 35 minutes until set.

Wheat-free crustless quiche

Chicken risotto

1 onion, peeled and diced
1 red pepper, deseeded and sliced
1 yellow pepper, deseeded and sliced
little olive oil for frying
1 x 250 g punnet button mushrooms, sliced
3 skinless, boneless chicken breasts, sliced thinly on the diagonal or leftover cooked chicken, skin removed

1–2 cloves garlic, crushed
2 cups arborio rice
1 cup white wine (optional)
6 cups chicken or vegetable stock
2 cups boiling water (if needed)
1 cup julienned carrots (optional)
salt and ground black pepper to taste

1. Sauté the onion and peppers in a little oil over a medium heat until glassy. Do not allow the onion to burn.
2. Turn up the heat and add the mushrooms. If using raw chicken breasts, add them at this point. Turn down the heat, add the garlic and stir for 1 minute.
3. Add a little more oil and the rice, and sauté. When the rice is coated, add the wine (if using) and the stock, ½ cup at a time, stirring until absorbed, before adding more. If necessary, add up to 2 cups of boiling water. If using leftover chicken, toss in when adding the last cup of liquid.
4. Add the carrots, then turn off the heat and allow to steam with the lid on for 5–10 minutes. Season to taste.
5. Serve on a platter with green beans or broccoli on the side.

EF; DF; WF; NF; SF; GF | Serves 4

Jacqui's 'favourite' chicken

My grown-up nieces still call this their favourite chicken. It is ridiculously easy to make and tastes really good.

8 chicken pieces (braai pack)
1 cup egg-free or tangy mayonnaise
1 cup smooth apricot jam

salt and ground black pepper to taste
sesame seeds to serve (optional)

1. Preheat the oven to 180 °C. Place the chicken pieces in a casserole dish.
2. Mix the mayonnaise and apricot jam, and pour over the chicken. Season to taste.
3. Bake uncovered for 1 hour, then cover with foil and bake for a further 30 minutes.
4. Sprinkle with sesame seeds if desired and serve with rice and a green salad – it's sticky, yummy and 'finger-licking good'!

DF; WF; NF; GF; alt EF | Serves 4–6

TIP: For a party, use just drumsticks or wings and serve on a platter.

Pineapple chicken

3 Tbsp sunflower oil

1 onion, peeled and chopped

2 cloves garlic, chopped or
  2 tsp crushed garlic

6 chicken breast fillets, sliced across the
  grain into strips

1 tsp sugar

4 Tbsp soy sauce or tamari (wheat-free
  soy sauce)

200 g fresh pineapple, peeled and cubed or
  1 x 440 g can pineapple pieces, drained

1 Tbsp grated fresh ginger or 1 tsp powdered

¼ cup water

salt and freshly ground black pepper to taste

1. Heat the oil in a large, heavy-bottomed frying pan or wok over a high heat. Add the onion and garlic and fry for 30 seconds. Then add the chicken pieces and stir-fry for a further minute.
2. Add the remaining ingredients and continue to stir-fry for 3–4 minutes until everything is cooked through.
3. Season to taste and serve hot with rice.

EF; DF; NF; alt WF; alt GF | Serves 4–6

Jacqui's 'favourite' chicken

Yummy curried chicken

This is an easy one-pot meal. My children enjoy the sweetness of the raisins. The sambals help make it a very social meal.

2 onions, peeled and finely chopped	1 tsp turmeric
1 clove garlic, crushed	¼ tsp ground ginger
2 Tbsp sunflower oil	¼ tsp ground cinnamon
1½ tsp mild–medium curry powder	2–3 bay leaves
16 chicken pieces	6 cups vegetable stock
1 cup seedless raisins	4–6 large carrots, peeled and cut into chunks
1½ cups pearl barley (optional)*	

1. In a pot, sauté the onions and garlic in the oil over a low heat until glassy. Add the curry powder and stir.
2. Turn up the heat, add the chicken pieces and brown.
3. Add the remaining ingredients, except the carrots, and bring to the boil. When boiling, turn down the heat and simmer for 1½ hours.
4. Add the carrots and cook for a further 30 minutes.
5. Serve with good white bread (for sopping up the gravy) and sambals: small bowls of chutney, sliced banana, desiccated coconut and chopped tomato, cucumber, onion, mango, pineapple and/or peach.

*If you leave out the barley (for those who are gluten intolerant), serve over brown or basmati rice.

EF; DF; WF; NF; SF; alt GF | Serves 8–10

TIP: This dish is really good if made in the morning. Allow to cool, skim off the fat and reheat in the evening for dinner. It freezes well, so make double for next week too!

Cooking is like love. It should be entered into with abandon or not at all.

Harriet van Horne

Yummy curried chicken

Rye pizza with tomato & basil

This recipe can be doubled and tripled easily. Leftover dough can be frozen for another day.

Pizza base:
1 cup warm water (not hot)
1 Tbsp sugar
1 x 10 g sachet instant dry yeast
¼ cup extra-virgin olive oil
1 tsp salt
1 x 500 g pkt rye flour (stoneground or fine)

Topping (per base):
1 x 125 g pkt Ina Paarman's Sundried Tomato Pesto
1 cup grated mozzarella cheese
1 cup halved cherry tomatoes seasoned with Ina Paarman's Green Onion Seasoning
a handful of fresh basil leaves, torn
oilve oil for drizzling

1. Mix the water and sugar in a large flat-bottomed bowl and sprinkle over the yeast. Leave for 5 minutes to prove, then add the oil and salt.
2. Add the flour, 1 cup at a time, and stir with a large spoon. The dough will become stiff and, when this happens, lightly knead it with floured hands. Rye flour has less elasticity than regular wheat flour, so gathering the dough and pushing it down will suffice. If the dough is very stiff, drizzle over an extra 1–2 Tbsp oil and lightly knead again. Leave the dough to rise for at least 1 hour, more if the weather is cold.
3. Preheat the oven to 180 °C. When hot, place two baking trays in the oven to heat.
4. When the dough has risen to about 1.5 times its size, punch it down and divide it in half. Place half onto a sheet of baking paper the size of your baking tray, cover with wax wrap and, pushing down with the heel of your hand, flatten the dough, working round and round until it is a largish rectangular shape. You can use a rolling pin dusted with maize meal to roll it flatter. Remove the wax wrap and repeat with the other half of the dough.
5. Place the flattened bases on their baking paper onto the warmed baking trays. Spread pesto over the bases, right to the edges, and bake for about 7 minutes until nicely puffed and just beginning to colour on the edges. Remove from the oven.
6. Sprinkle the cheese over the bases and dot with the seasoned tomato halves. Add some torn basil leaves before baking and the rest after.
7. Drizzle with olive oil and bake each pizza for 10 minutes until the bases are nicely browned and crisp.

WF; EF | Makes 2 medium-sized thin-based pizzas

Polenta 'pizza'

This is a good wheat-free alternative. Although nothing like a regular pizza base, it's still very tasty.

Pizza base:
2½ cups water
½ tsp salt
1 cup polenta
olive oil for drizzling
crushed garlic to taste
cracked black pepper to taste

Topping options:
2–3 Tbsp Ina Paarman's Sundried Tomato
    Pesto or any tomato pasta/pizza sauce
1 cup grated mozzarella or ½ cup grated
    mozzarella + ½ cup grated Cheddar
pitted olives, roasted vegetables, cubed feta
    cheese, sliced bananas, shredded spinach,
    caramelised onions, canned tuna, etc.

1. Preheat the oven to 180 °C. Grease a baking tray or line with baking paper.
2. Bring the water and salt to the boil in a pot. Whisk in the polenta, then stir for 1 minute. Remove from the heat and whisk to remove any lumps.
3. Spread a thin layer of polenta (about 2 cm thick) over the base of the greased or lined baking tray. Drizzle over a little olive oil, sprinkle with crushed garlic and grind over some black pepper. Bake for 25–30 minutes until firm.
4. Remove from the oven and spread over the pesto or tomato sauce. Sprinkle over the cheese and add toppings of your choice. Bake for 5–10 minutes, then remove from the oven and allow to cool. Make sure the polenta is cooked through; it will firm up when it cools. Cut into squares and pile on a platter to serve.

WF; GF; SF; NF | Serves 2

Polenta 'pizza'

Pasta with oven-
roasted vegetables

Macaroni egg

This easy, one-dish meal comes with wheat- gluten- and dairy-free options.

1 x 500 g pkt wheat- or gluten-free macaroni
6 large eggs
½ cup soy/rice/cow's milk
1 tsp herb salt

freshly ground black pepper to taste
paprika to taste
grated cheese for topping (optional)

1. Preheat the oven to 160 °C. Cook the pasta according to the packet instructions until al dente. Drain and place in a greased casserole dish.
2. Whisk the eggs with the milk, salt and pepper, and pour over the pasta. Sprinkle over some paprika.
3. Bake for 50–60 minutes until the egg is set and the top crisped. If using cheese, sprinkle on top and return to the oven until the cheese is melted and bubbling.

NF; alt DF; alt WF; alt GF | Serves 4–6

TIP: Layer the base of the casserole dish with thinly sliced onions and top the pasta with thinly sliced tomatoes or halved cherry tomatoes for good iron absorption.

Pasta with oven-roasted vegetables

1 large butternut, peeled and cubed
2 large red onions, peeled and cut
   into wedges
2 Tbsp olive oil
1 tsp freshly ground black pepper
1 x 500 g pkt wheat/corn/rice fusilli or penne

2 Tbsp water
salt and ground black pepper to taste
2 Tbsp pine nuts, toasted (optional)
½–1 cup wild rocket leaves
balsamic vinegar for drizzling
1 tsp chopped dried rosemary for sprinkling

1. Preheat the oven to 200 °C.
2. Place the butternut and onions in a large roasting pan, drizzle with the oil and season with the pepper. Roast for 40–45 minutes or until the vegetables are soft and slightly caramelised.
3. Meanwhile, cook the pasta according to the packet instructions. Drain and return to the pot.
4. Add the roast vegetables and water. Mix and heat rapidly until just warm. Season with salt and pepper.
5. Serve on warmed plates, topped with the pine nuts (if using) and rocket, drizzled with balsamic vinegar and sprinkled with chopped dried rosemary.

DF; alt WF; alt GF; alt NF | Serves 4–6

TIP: Toasted sunflower seeds can be substituted for the pine nuts as a more economical option.

Butternut & goat's cheese pasta

Thanks to my friend, Gill de Bruyn, for this. We enjoyed it with a bottle of red wine on a rainy Seattle afternoon!

1 butternut, peeled and cubed
3–4 whole cloves garlic, unpeeled
1 onion, peeled and sliced
3–4 sprigs of rosemary
2–3 tsp sugar

2–3 Tbsp olive oil
1 x 500 g pkt durum wheat/rye fettuccine
1 Tbsp butter or olive oil
1 x 100 g log chevin (goat's milk cheese)
salt and ground black pepper to taste

1. Preheat the oven to 180 °C. Spray a roasting pan with non-stick cooking spray or coat with oil.
2. Place the butternut, garlic and onion in the pan with the rosemary sprigs. Sprinkle over the sugar and drizzle with the olive oil. Bake for 30–45 minutes until the butternut is cooked through and starting to brown. Remove from the oven.
3. Cook the pasta according to the packet instructions until al dente. Drain and place in a serving dish. Dot the pasta with the butter or olive oil.
4. Squeeze out the garlic paste from the cloves and toss with the pasta, then top with the butternut and onions. Crumble over the cheese, season to taste and sprinkle over some extra rosemary. Serve with a green salad, garlic bread and a good red wine!

EF; NF; SF; alt WF; alt GF | Serves 4

Monkey-gland minute steaks

Quick and easy to prepare, this dish is always popular. The recipe can be successfully doubled and tripled. Keep extra marinade in a sealed jar in the fridge. It's excellent for basting chops or ribs.

6 minute steaks
salt and ground black pepper to taste
olive oil for frying
3 onions, peeled and thinly sliced
1 tsp crushed garlic

Monkey gland:
1 cup tomato purée
1 cup mild chutney
¼ cup Worcestershire sauce
¼ cup olive oil

1. Preheat the oven to 180 °C. Season the steaks with salt and pepper and brown in some olive oil in a frying pan. Remove the steaks with a slotted spoon and place in a casserole dish.
2. Add the onions and garlic to the same pan and sauté until soft and glassy. Pour over the steaks.
3. Mix the marinade ingredients well and pour over the meat. Cover and allow to slow cook for 1 hour.
4. Serve hot with boiled baby potatoes.

DF; WF; GF; NF; EF | Serves 6

Butternut & goat's
cheese pasta

Steamed bobotie spinach rolls

1 Tbsp olive oil
2 onions, peeled and finely chopped
500 g lean beef or lamb mince
1 x 410 g can baked beans in tomato sauce or
    1 x 410 g can butter beans, drained
1 ripe tomato, chopped
1 clove garlic, crushed
1 tsp chopped fresh ginger
1½ tsp turmeric

2 tsp cumin
½ tsp cayenne pepper
2 Tbsp seedless raisins
1 Tbsp apricot jam
2 Tbsp almond flakes, toasted (optional)
salt and ground black pepper to taste
12 large spinach leaves, washed well
12 toothpicks

1. Preheat the oven to 180 °C.
2. Heat the oil in a frying pan over a medium heat and sauté the onions until soft. Without adding extra oil, add the mince and cook until lightly browned. Reduce the heat and add the beans, tomato, garlic, ginger and spices, and simmer until the meat is cooked. Then mix in the raisins, jam and almonds (if using). Season with salt and pepper to taste. Remove from the heat and allow to cool slightly.
3. Place 2–3 Tbsp of the mince filling in the centre of the top third of each spinach leaf. Fold in the sides, then roll up from the top. Secure each roll with a toothpick. If you are serving these as a starter, you can reduce the amount of filling.
4. Handling them carefully so they don't break, place the rolls in a casserole dish. Cover with foil or a lid and bake for 10–15 minutes – the rolls will steam inside the dish.
5. Serve on a bed of brown or white rice, accompanied by small side dishes of chutney, desiccated coconut and a choice of sambals (see below).

DF; WF; GF; EF; alt NF | Serves 4–6

TIP: You can substitute cabbage leaves for the spinach. If using cabbage leaves, microwave them for 10–20 seconds to soften before using.

Sambals

Yoghurt sambal:
Mix 1 cup plain yoghurt, ½ cup grated English cucumber, ¼ tsp cumin, ¼ tsp salt, ¼ tsp sugar and a twist of black pepper.

Onion sambal
Mix 2 sliced large onions, 2 finely chopped chillies, 2 Tbsp vinegar, a pinch of salt and 1 Tbsp chopped fresh coriander or parsley.

Banana sambal
Slice 2 firm ripe bananas into discs and sprinkle over 2 Tbsp desiccated coconut.

Tomato Sambal
Mix 2–3 chopped and deseeded firm ripe Israeli or roma tomatoes, ½ diced English cucumber, 1 diced red onion and a pinch of salt and pepper.

Yummy cottage pie

For 'night-shade' allergies (i.e. allergy to potato, tomato, capsicum, aubergine, etc.) use a sweet-potato topping and eliminate the tomato. This recipe makes four pies, one for tonight and three to freeze. But freeze prior to topping with potato. Defrost, top with potato and bake as directed. Or simply divide the ingredients by four.

3 kg lean beef mince
2 Tbsp sunflower oil
3–4 onions, peeled and chopped
3–4 table celery stalks, chopped
4 carrots, peeled and chopped or grated
2 cloves garlic, crushed
1 cup seedless raisins (optional)
1 cup chopped dried apricots (optional)
1 cup tomato purée or 1 cup chutney

1 Tbsp herb salt
1 tsp prepared mustard
1 cup oat bran
2 x 410 g cans baked beans in tomato sauce
    or 2 x 410 g cans kidney beans (no sauce)
salt and freshly ground black pepper to taste
3 large sweet potatoes or 5 potatoes, boiled
    and mashed with ½ cup soy/rice milk

1. In a large pan, brown the mince in batches in the oil. Remove with a slotted spoon into a separate pot.
2. In the same pan, sauté the onions, celery, carrots and garlic until wilted and glazed. Add the raisins and apricots (if using), the tomato purée or chutney, herb salt and mustard. Add this to the pot with the meat, mix well and bring to the boil on the stove. Reduce the heat to low and simmer for 1½ hours.
3. Remove from the heat and stir in the oat bran and beans. Season to taste. Divide the mixture between four casserole dishes. Preheat the oven to 180 °C.
4. When the dishes are cool, cover and freeze three of them. Top the fourth with the mashed potato and bake for 30 minutes. Then turn on the grill and bake for a further 5–10 minutes to crisp the potato.
4. Serve with a green salad, broccoli or green beans.

NF; EF; DF; WF; GF | Serves 5–6

Lamb stew

Lamb stew

Lamb is easily digested and therefore good for people with allergies.

1 kg stewing lamb
olive oil for frying
2 onions, peeled and chopped
2 tsp crushed garlic
1 tsp dried rosemary
½ tsp ground ginger
½ tsp cumin
¼ tsp ground cinnamon

¼ tsp turmeric
2–3 cups chicken or vegetable stock
4 carrots, peeled and cut into chunks
3–4 baby marrows, sliced into chunks or
  1 cup frozen peas
2 large sweet potatoes or 3 large potatoes,
  peeled and cubed
salt and ground black pepper to taste

1. In a medium-sized pot, brown the lamb in a little oil. Remove with a slotted spoon and set aside.
2. Lower the heat and add the onions and garlic. When the onion is glazed and transparent, add the rosemary and spices, and stir-fry for a further 1 minute. Add the meat and stock, and bring to the boil.
3. Lower the heat and simmer for 1 hour. Add the remaining vegetables, season to taste and cook for a further 30 minutes. Serve with basmati rice.

DF; WF; GF; NF; EF; SF | Serves 4–6

Lentil curry with brown rice

2–3 Tbsp olive oil
1 large onion, peeled and finely chopped
2 tsp mild–medium curry powder
½ tsp ground ginger or 1 tsp grated fresh
¼ tsp ground cinnamon
¼ tsp cumin
2 bay leaves
2 cups brown lentils, rinsed (do not soak)
1 tsp crushed garlic

4 carrots, peeled and diced
2 potatoes, peeled and diced
2 sweet potatoes, peeled and diced
2–3 baby marrows, sliced
1 cup frozen peas
1 cup frozen corn
4 cups vegetable stock
2 cups brown rice, rinsed
salt and ground black pepper to taste

1. Heat the oil in a pot and sauté the onion, then lower the heat, add the curry powder and spices, and stir.
2. Add the lentils, garlic and vegetables, and stir to coat. Pour over the stock, bring to the boil and simmer for 45 minutes or until the lentils are cooked through. If necessary, add a further 1 cup water.
3. While this is cooking, place the rice in a separate pot with 6 cups water. Bring to the boil and simmer until all the liquid has been absorbed.
4. Season the curry and serve with the brown rice and a selection of sambals (see page 68).

NF; DF; WF; GF; SF | Serves 4

Lemon & mint 'ice cream' (page 76)

Dessert should close the meal gently and not in a pyrotechnic blaze of glory.
No cultivated feeder, already well fed, thanks his host for confronting
him with a dessert so elaborate that not to eat it is simply rude –
like refusing to watch one's host blow up Bloomingdale's.

Alan Koehler, *Madison Avenue Cook Book*

Desserts

Finish your meal on a sweet note with dessert. Love and sweetness go together. 'Honey', 'Sweetiepie', 'Sugar' – we use these words as terms of endearment for the people we love most. Love is sweet and it's no wonder that our celebrations are never complete without puddings, pies, ice creams and sugary treats. What would holidays and birthdays be without bountiful displays of desserts?

But there is rigor in making a dessert. Good baking is exact and indebted to science. We may roughly chop a potato for a stew, but desserts and cakes are made with care, to later be embellished with swirls, mint leaves, whipped cream and, sometimes, more sugar. A swirl takes effort, as does the exact placement of a leaf, but a beautifully presented, delicious and mouth-watering dessert is worth it!

Roasted nectarines

6 nectarines, halved and stoned   ½ cup brown sugar
125 g margarine or butter, cut up

1. Switch on the oven's grill and grease a casserole dish.
2. Place the nectarine halves face up in the casserole dish.
3. Dot each half with the margarine or butter and sprinkle over the brown sugar.
4. Place under the grill until browned and bubbly.
5. Serve warm with vanilla ice cream, whipped cream or Orley Whip™ non-dairy cream.

EF; NF; GF; WF; alt DF | Serves 6

TIP: You can do the same with sliced bananas, but sprinkle with cinnamon before roasting.

Oven-stewed apples & pears

6 Golden Delicious or Granny Smith apples   1–2 cups water
3 pears   1 cup brown sugar
1 x 250 g pkt seedless raisins   1 tsp ground cinnamon

1. Preheat the oven to 180 °C. Grease a casserole dish.
2. Core and thickly slice the apples and pears (do not peel). Place the apples, pears and raisins in the casserole dish and pour over enough water to submerge, but not cover completely. Sprinkle over the sugar and cinnamon.
3. Cover with foil and bake for 45 minutes. Then remove the foil and return to the oven for a further 30 minutes, or longer if need be. The fruit should be lightly browned and the water mostly cooked away to leave a thickish syrup in the bottom of the dish.
4. Serve hot or cold with vanilla ice cream, whipped cream or Orley Whip™ non-dairy cream.

EF; DF; GF; WF; NF | Serves 6

Mango frozen dessert

4 large mangoes, peeled, deseeded
   and cubed
1 cup sugar or ¾ cup fructose
1 cup cream or soy cream

1 cup ice
2 Tbsp lemon juice
zest of 1 lemon

1. Place the mangoes, sugar, cream, ice and lemon juice in a blender and purée until smooth.
2. Pour into a large resealable freezer bag and freeze for 1 hour, removing the bag from the freezer every 15 minutes or so to mush the contents around.
3. To serve, cut the corner off the bag and squeeze directly into bowls. Decorate with the lemon zest.

EF; WF; GF; NF; alt DF; alt SF | Serves 6

Lemon & mint 'ice cream'

This is a light and refreshing dessert.

4 eggs, separated
1 cup caster sugar
juice and zest of 2 large lemons

2 x 125 ml sachets Orley Whip™ non-dairy
   cream or 1 cup whipping cream
½ cup finely chopped fresh mint

1. Lightly grease a mould or round cake tin and set aside.
2. Beat the egg whites until just beginning to stiffen, then beat in the caster sugar, a little at a time, until the whites are peaking.
3. In a separate bowl, whisk the lemon juice and zest with the cream until peaking. Fold in the chopped mint.
4. Lightly beat the egg yolks and fold into the egg-white mixture. Then fold in the cream mixture.
5. Spoon into the greased mould or tin, cover with clingfilm and freeze for at least 4 hours before serving.

WF; NF; GF; alt DF | Serves 6

Coffee 'ice cream'

2 extra-large eggs, separated
½ cup sugar
4 heaped tsp instant coffee

2 x 125 ml sachets Orley Whip™
non-dairy cream
chocolate curls or sprinkles to decorate

1. Lightly grease a loaf tin and set aside.
2. Beat the egg whites until just stiff (do not overbeat). Set aside.
3. In a separate bowl, beat the egg yolks with the sugar and instant coffee. Fold this into the egg whites using a spatula.
4. Beat the Orley Whip™ until stiff and fold this into the mixture.
5. Pour into the greased tin, cover with clingfilm and freeze for 6 hours or overnight.
6. Just before serving, unmould onto a platter and decorate with chocolate curls or sprinkles. This is delicious served with no-bake chocolate clusters (see page 100).

DF; NF; WF; GF | Serves 4–6

Banana frozen dessert

½ cup cold rice/coconut/cow's milk
1 tsp vanilla essence
1 tsp cocoa powder

½ cup almonds (optional)
3 ripe bananas, peeled, sliced into chunks
and frozen the day before

1. In a blender, combine the milk, vanilla essence, cocoa powder and almonds (if using).
2. Add the frozen banana slices and blend until smooth, but still firm.
3. Eat immediately. This gets very hard when refrozen.

SF; EF; WF; GF; alt NF; alt DF | Serves 3–4

*My therapist told me the way to achieve true inner peace is to finish what I start. So far today,
I have finished two bags of M&Ms and a chocolate cake. I feel better already.*

Dave Barry

Telephone pudding

125 g margarine, softened
1 cup sugar
1 extra-large egg
1 tsp ground ginger
1 tsp bicarbonate of soda
2 Tbsp apricot jam
1½ cups self-raising flour
¼–½ cup soy milk

Syrup
2 cups boiling water
1 cup sugar

Orley Whip™ non-dairy cream or soy
    pouring cream to serve

1. Preheat the oven to 180 °C. Lightly grease a large ovenproof dish.
2. Cream the margarine and sugar until pale and fluffy. Add the egg and beat well, then add the ginger, bicarbonate of soda and jam.
3. Sift in the flour and beat well. Add enough milk to make a soft, dropping consistency. Set aside.
4. To make the syrup, combine the boiling water with the sugar in a pot over a medium heat, sitrring until the sugar has dissolved. Pour onto the base of the greased ovenproof dish and spoon in the batter.
5. Cover with a lid or foil and bake for 10 minutes. Then uncover and continue to bake for 50 minutes. The pudding should be firm and slightly brown with a syrupy sauce underneath. Serve hot with non-dairy cream.

DF; NF; YF | Serves 8

Malva pudding

1 x 410 g can fruit cocktail
2 cups self-raising flour
1 cup sugar
2 tsp bicarbonate of soda
1 tsp salt
2 extra-large eggs

Sauce
¾ cup sugar
1 tsp vanilla essence
1 x 125 ml sachet Orley Whip™
    non-dairy cream
1 Tbsp oil

1. Preheat the oven to 180 °C. Grease a casserole or pie dish.
2. In a large bowl, mix all of the batter ingredients, including the syrup from the fruit cocktail.
3. Spoon the batter into the greased dish and bake for 30 minutes or until browned.
4. Whisk together the sauce ingredients. Using a kebab stick or toothpick, poke about 30 holes in the cooked cake and pour over the sauce while the cake is still hot. Serve hot or at room temperature.

DF; NF; YF | Serves 8–10

Egg-less fruit 'mousse'

This recipe is extremely easy and cost-effective to make, but allow time for the jelly to set. This can be made the day before.

2 x 125 ml sachets Orley Whip™
   non-dairy cream
2 x 80 g boxes peach jelly (or any flavour)

1 cup peach juice
1 x 410 g can sliced peaches, drained and
   syrup reserved

1. In a medium-sized bowl, beat the Orley Whip™ until peaks form and set aside in the fridge.
2. Make up 1 box of jelly according to the packet instructions, but substitute the peach juice for 1 cup water. Whisk well and set aside for 10 minutes to cool.
3. Reserve 2 peach slices for decoration and place the rest in the bottom of a serving bowl.
4. Make up the second box of jelly according to the packet instructions, but substitute 1 cup reserved peach syrup for 1 cup water and pour over the peaches. Place in the fridge to set.
5. Remove the Orley Whip™ from the fridge and fold in the first box of jelly using a spatula. Place this in the fridge to set.
6. When everything is set, spoon the Orley Whip™ mixture over the jelly/peach combo and decorate with the reserved peach slices.

DF; EF; WF; GF; NF | Serves 6

Pineapple ginger tart

2 cups self-raising flour
a pinch of salt
1 tsp ground ginger
1 cup sugar
1 cup oil

1 extra-large egg or 2 tsp Orgran No Egg
   powder mixed with 2 Tbsp hot water
1 x 820 g can pineapple rings, drained and
   1 cup syrup reserved
extra ground ginger for sprinkling

1. Preheat the oven to 180 °C. Grease a pie dish.
2. Sift the flour, salt, ginger and sugar into a large bowl.
3. Pour in the oil, egg or egg substitute and 1 cup reserved pineapple syrup and mix well.
4. Place the drained pineapple rings on the bottom of the greased dish, spoon over the batter and sprinkle with a little extra ground ginger.
5. Bake for 25–30 minutes, until a toothpick inserted in the centre comes out clean and the top is nicely browned.

DF; NF; alt EF | Serves 8

Decadent wheat-free peach crumble

Apple crumble

4 Golden Delicious apples, unpeeled, cored and thickly sliced
½ cup apple juice mixed with ½ cup water
1 cup oats
1 cup cornflakes

1 cup Oatees
1 cup sugar
½ cup sunflower oil
a pinch of salt
½ tsp ground cinnamon

1. Preheat the oven to 180 °C. Grease a round quiche dish.
2. Place the apple slices on the bottom of the greased dish, pour over the apple juice mixture and bake for 30 minutes until the apples are soft. Remove from the oven.
3. Combine the oats, cornflakes, Oatees, sugar, oil and salt, and spoon over the apples. Sprinkle with the cinnamon and bake for 45–60 minutes until crispy on top.
4. Serve with non-dairy whipped cream or vanilla ice cream. This recipe doubles easily.

EF; WF; NF; DF | Serves 8–10

Decadent wheat-free peach crumble

1 x 820 g can peach halves, drained and syrup reserved
1½ cups rice/barley flour
½ cup almond meal (pulse 1 cup raw or toasted almonds until powdery)
½ tsp ground cinnamon
¼ tsp ground ginger
¼ tsp salt

1 tsp baking powder
1 egg or 2 tsp Orgran No Egg powder mixed with 2 Tbsp hot water
1 cup oil
1 tsp vanilla essence
1 cup reserved peach syrup mixed with ½ cup sugar
1 Tbsp icing sugar

1. Preheat the oven to 180 °C. Grease a small casserole or pie dish well.
2. Place the peaches cut-side down in the greased dish and set aside.
3. Whisk together the dry ingredients. In a separate bowl, whisk together the egg, oil, vanilla essence and syrup-sugar mixture. Make a well in the centre of the dry mixture and pour in the liquid mixture, stirring until just blended. Spoon over the peaches and sprinkle with a little extra ground cinnamon.
4. Bake for 35 minutes or until a toothpick inserted in the centre comes out clean. Sift over the icing sugar and serve warm or at room temperature with vanilla ice cream or non-dairy whipped cream.
5. Alternatively, bake in a small round or square baking tin lined with baking paper. Invert the baked cake onto a platter and you have an 'upside-down cake' with the fruit on top.

WF; DF; alt EF; alt GF | Serves 8–10

Party box

IT'S PARTY TIME … Help! Isn't this how all of us with allergies feel? Every time I sent Lennie to a party he would come home feeling awful and spend the next day off school with a rash, upset tummy, etc. Not to mention Sam, who would feel sad and deprived at every party. We hit rock bottom when they received invitations to four parties spaced over two weeks. I envisioned sick kids and a crazy mother. Enter the solution: Give an incentive and be prepared! Instead of getting a party

Cakes
& bakes

pack at the party, we take our own. Keep a stock of paper packets or small party boxes, and have your child decorate it before filling it. Fill the box with safe treats (I keep a stock of allergy-friendly baked items in the freezer and some 'safe' chips in the cupboard) and a drink, and fill the gap with bits and pieces like fruit sticks, popcorn and dried fruit. Remember that even the most disciplined person is going to feel like something that's not perfectly 'healthy', so add a dairy-free chocolate, some candy (e.g. sparkles) or anything else that fits the dietary 'budget' so to speak. I give Lennie Flings or corn chips instead of the (innocuous to some) dreaded potato chip. We discuss the self-control aspect and use a star chart to earn a much-desired non-food treat. Being prepared works for adults too; people won't mind if you offer to bring along a plate of cookies to share or a container of food that's 'safe' . It takes the pressure off of them and it makes for being a 'good' guest too!

Brenda's banana bread

2 cups rolled oats
2 Tbsp honey
125 g butter or light olive oil
about 12 pitted dates, soaked and chopped
2 cups mashed ripe banana

½ cup soya flour
½ cup rice flour
2 tsp baking powder
½ cup soy/rice milk

1. Preheat the oven to 160 °C. Lightly grease a loaf tin and line with baking paper.
2. In a blender, pulse the oats to a fine powder, then add the remaining ingredients and blend. The batter should have a dropping consistency; add water or more milk if necessary.
3. Pour the batter into the greased loaf tin and bake for 60 minutes or until a skewer inserted into the centre comes out clean. Remove from the oven and allow to stand for 5 minutes before carefully turning out onto a wire rack. Serve warm or at room temperature.

EF; WF; alt DF

Melissa's egg-free scones

1 cup cake flour
1½ tsp baking powder
a pinch of salt

3 Tbsp oil
⅓ cup water

1. Preheat the oven to 200 °C. Lightly grease a muffin pan.
2. Mix the flour, baking powder and salt, and set aside.
3. In a separate bowl, whisk together the oil and water. Add this to the dry mixture and blend well.
4. Fill the greased muffin holes until three-quarters full.
5. Bake for 12–15 minutes.

EF; NF; DF; SF | Makes 6

TIP: For a sweeter 'rock bun'-type scone, add ¼ cup sugar and ¼ cup seedless raisins to the batter. Sprinkle with sugar before baking.
For a more savoury variety, substitute ½ tsp herb salt for the salt and serve with grated cheese or sheese (soy cheese).

Easy banana cake

1 cup sugar

¼ cup dairy-free margarine

½ Tbsp oil

¼ cup water

1 tsp vanilla essence

1 cup mashed ripe banana

1½ cups cake flour or ½ cup rice flour +
  ½ cup rye flour + ½ cup maize meal

1½ tsp bicarbonate of soda (or 2 tsp if using
  wheat-free flour)

1. Preheat the oven to 180 °C. Grease and line a small round cake tin or a loaf tin.
2. Cream the sugar and margarine. Add the oil, water, vanilla essence and mashed banana, and stir.
3. Combine the flour and bicarbonate of soda, and add to the banana mixture. Stir briskly until just blended.
4. Spoon the batter into the greased tin and bake for 50 minutes. Remove from the oven and allow to stand for 5 minutes before carefully turning out onto a wire rack to cool.
5. Sift over some icing sugar when cooled or ice with non-dairy whipped cream and top with walnuts.

`EF; NF; DF; alt WF`

Vegan vanilla cake

2½ cups cake flour

2½ tsp baking powder

¼ tsp salt

1 cup sugar

½ cup oil

1 tsp vanilla essence

200 ml soy/rice milk or water

Butter icing

½ cup dairy-free margarine

1 cup icing sugar, sifted

½ tsp vanilla essence

1. Preheat the oven to 190 °C. Grease and line a small cake tin.
2. Sift the flour, baking powder, salt and sugar together. Add the oil, vanilla essence and milk, and mix until just blended.
3. Spoon the batter into the greased tin and bake for 30 minutes. Carefully turn out onto a wire rack to cool.
4. To make the icing, mix the margarine and icing sugar, and add the vanilla essence. Smooth onto the cooled cake using a spatula or butter knife.

`EF; DF; NF`

VARIATIONS: Sweet and light lemon cake: add ¼ cup lemon juice in place of ¼ cup of the milk or water. Add 1 tsp lemon juice to the icing and sprinkle lemon zest over the iced cake.
Orange cake: add 1 cup orange juice instead of the milk or water and reduce the sugar to ½ cup. Add 1 tsp orange juice to the icing and sprinkle orange zest over the iced cake.
Apple cake: slice 1 or 2 pie apples and lay the slices on top of the cooled cake. Sprinkle with cinnamon sugar.

CHOCOLATE CAKES

I feel I should name this section 'Ode to the Chocolate Cake'. Seriously though, we all love chocolate cake and I just could not choose between these delicious recipes, they are all so good! My family really enjoyed taste-testing them and would have endorsed me to add a few extra to the book. These are the best of the bunch…

Black forest cake

2 cups barley flour or 1 cup barley flour
   mixed with 1 cup rice flour
1 cup rye flour
1 cup maize meal
1 cup cocoa powder
¾ cup fructose or 1 cup sugar
1 heaped Tbsp Orgran No Egg powder
   (unmixed) or 2 extra-large eggs
4 tsp baking powder
1 cup soy milk

¼ cup sunflower oil
2 cups boiling water
2 tsp vanilla essence
1 x 425 g can black cherries, drained or
   1 cup fresh strawberries/blueberries
1 x 250 ml box Orley Whip™ non-dairy cream

Chocolate ganache
½–1 cup carob chunks or chocolate chips
¼ cup soy milk

1. Preheat the oven to 160 °C. Grease and line a square brownie tin or 2 round cake tins.
2. Combine the flours, maize meal, cocoa powder, fructose or sugar, Orgran No Egg powder and baking powder in a large bowl and whisk very well.
3. In a separate bowl, combine the soy milk, oil, water and vanilla essence, and mix. If using fresh eggs, lightly whisk and then blend into the milk mixture.
4. Make a well in the centre of the dry ingredients and pour in the milk mixture. Stir with a whisk until just blended. The consistency should be that of a thick batter.
5. Pour into the greased tin/s and bake for 40 minutes, or until a toothpick inserted in the centre comes out clean. While the cake is baking, whip the non-dairy cream until peaks form and refrigerate. Pour the black cherries into a colander to drain.
6. Remove the cake from the oven and leave to stand for 10 minutes. Turn out carefully onto a wire rack and, when almost cool, transfer to a serving platter.
7. To make the ganache, place the carob chunks or chocolate chips and soy milk in a small saucepan and warm over a low heat. Stir to blend, until the carob or chocolate has melted. Alternatively, microwave for 30 seconds on high. Stir and return to the microwave for a further 30 seconds.
8. For a single-layer cake, pour the ganache onto the warm cake and smooth it with a spatula or the back of a spoon. It will form a 'puddle' around the cake. Leave to cool. When cooled, top with the whipped cream and decorate with the cherries. For double-layer cake, smooth the whipped cream over one layer. Place the cherries evenly over the cream and place the second layer on top. Pour the ganache over the top, smooth over and serve with a cup of really good filter coffee – heavenly!

WF; DF; alt EF; alt SF

Black forest cake

The ultimate egg-free cupcakes

4 cups cake flour
4 tsp baking powder
3 Tbsp cocoa powder
2 cups sugar
1 cup sunflower or canola oil

1 Tbsp vinegar
2 tsp vanilla essence
1½ cups hot plain water or mixed with a
   spoon or two of instant coffee (optional)

1. Preheat the oven to 180 °C. Fill 2 muffin pans with cupcake papers.
2. Sift the flour, baking powder and cocoa powder into a large bowl. Add the sugar and sift a second time.
3. In a separate bowl, whisk together the oil, vinegar, vanilla essence and water or coffee.
4. Make a well in the centre of the dry ingredients, add the wet ingredients and mix until just combined. Spoon the batter into the cupcake papers using a small ladle or big dessertspoon.
5. Bake for 30–35 minutes until a toothpick inserted in the centres comes out clean. Turn out onto a wire rack to cool before icing (see below). These egg-free cupcakes will not rise as much as those containing eggs, but taste just as good!

EF; DF; NF | Makes 24

TIP: For a more formal dessert, turn the cupcakes upside down and serve grouped together on a cake stand or individually plated. Spoon over some dark chocolate 'sauce' (see topping for the chocolate fudge cake opposite) and decorate with rose petals.

Bright 'butter' icing

2 cups icing sugar
1 cup dairy-free margarine
½ tsp vanilla essence (optional)

½ tsp gel food colouring (available from
   speciality baking shops) or 1–2 tsp liquid
   food colouring (colour of your choice)

1. Using a blender or whisk, blend all of the ingredients at high speed to achieve a fluffy, light icing.
2. Using a butter knife, thickly spread the icing in a 'fluffing' motion onto the cooled cupcakes.
3. Get creative and top each cupcake with flower petals, multi-coloured sprinkles, Smarties, Jelly Tots or small plastic toys, such as butterflies.

EF; DF; NF; WF; GF

Chocolate fudge cake

This cake bakes best in a bundt pan, but a loaf tin can also be used.

1¾ cups cake flour
4 Tbsp cocoa powder
2 tsp baking powder
½ tsp salt
⅓ cup sunflower oil
1 tsp vanilla essence
1½ cups sugar

1½ cups hot water

Chocolate topping
100 g dark chocolate (preferably cooking chocolate or chocolate with a high cocoa content of 70% and up)
¼ cup soy milk

1. Preheat the oven to 180 °C. Grease a bundt pan or loaf tin and set aside.
2. Sift the flour, cocoa powder, baking powder and salt into a bowl and set aside.
3. In a mixer or using a whisk, mix the oil and vanilla essence. Add the sugar, ½ cup at a time, blending well.
4. Add the dry ingredients, alternately with the water. Beat well.
5. Pour the batter into the greased pan/tin and bake immediately for 35–40 minutes, until a skewer inserted in the centre comes out clean.
6. When done, carefully remove from the oven. Do not bang it down on the counter, as the cake will flop. Leave to stand for 5 minutes, before turning out carefully onto a wire rack to cool. When cooled, transfer to a cake stand. As this cake has no egg binder, it is delicate, so treat it gently.
7. In a double-boiler or in the microwave, melt the chocolate and stir in the milk. Whisk until smooth and then spoon over the cooled cake while still warm.

`EF; DF; NF`

TIP: Here's a good tip my sister Jacqui got from the doyenne of cooking, Ina Paarman: If you want to make a cake mix that requires eggs, but can't use eggs, substitute 1 tsp white vinegar for each egg (up to a maximum of 3 tsp) and bake as usual. Cupcakes will rise a little less and cakes will be softer (more fragile), but you won't taste the vinegar!

People think it's impossible to make a cake without eggs or wheat or any of the commonly used and known ingredients. Well, in the words of Lewis Carroll … 'Why, sometimes I've believed as many as six impossible things before breakfast.'

Tammi Forman

Easy yummy brownies

Easy yummy brownies

1 cup barley/soya flour
1 cup rice flour
1 cup rye/millet flour or almond meal
1 cup maize meal
1 cup cocoa powder
1½ cups sugar or 1¼ cups fructose
4 tsp baking powder
1 heaped Tbsp Orgran No Egg powder
 (unmixed) or 2 large eggs

1 cup soy milk
¼ cup sunflower oil
2 tsp vanilla essence
2 cups black coffee
icing sugar for dusting

Chocolate sauce
½ cup dark chocolate chunks or chips
¼ cup soy milk

1. Preheat the oven to 160 °C. Grease and line a rectangular casserole dish or 2 brownie tins.
2. Combine the flours, maize meal, cocoa powder, sugar or fructose, baking powder and Orgran No Egg powder in a large bowl and whisk.
3. In a separate bowl, combine the soy milk, oil, vanilla essence and coffee, and mix. If using fresh eggs, lightly whisk and then blend into the coffee mixture.
4. Make a well in centre of the dry ingredients and pour in the coffee mixture. Stir with a whisk until just blended. The consistency should be that of a thick batter.
5. Pour the batter into the greased dish or tins and bake for 40–50 minutes, or until a toothpick inserted in the centre comes out clean and the cake pulls away from the sides. Remove from the oven and leave to stand for 10 minutes.
6. Invert the cake onto a wire rack and carefully remove the baking paper, then flip the cake onto a serving platter. With a skewer or toothpick poke about 20 holes in the cake. This will allow the sauce to seep into the brownies.
7. Make the chocolate sauce. Place the chocolate chunks or chips and soy milk in a bowl and microwave for 30 seconds on high. Stir and return to the microwave for a further 30 seconds or until the chocolate has melted. Stir well to blend. Alternatively, use a small saucepan over a low heat on the stove.
8. Pour the sauce over the warm cake and smooth over. Cut into squares or triangles and sift over a little icing sugar just before serving. For a yummy dessert, serve with a dollop of vanilla ice cream and a smooth espresso.

DF; alt WF; alt NF; alt GF; alt SF; alt EF | Makes about 16

TIP: Gluten-free flours respond better to using real eggs, if possible, to bind.

Easy egg-free chocolate cake

This cake has a light crumbly texture and is delicious! You won't taste the vinegar: it does the work of the eggs, binding the cake nicely.

1½ cups cake flour
½ cup cocoa powder
1 tsp bicarbonate of soda
½ tsp salt
1 cup sugar
½ cup vegetable oil

1 cup cold water or cold coffee
2 tsp vanilla essence
2 tsp vinegar
frozen cherries/raspberries/
    cranberries (optional)

1. Preheat the oven to 190 °C.
2. Combine all of the dry ingredients in a small brownie-sized pan (no greasing required).
3. In a separate bowl, whisk the oil, water or coffee and vanilla essence. Add this to the dry ingredients and stir until mixed.
4. Add the vinegar and quickly stir in. If you would like, put some frozen berries on top of the batter before baking. Bake immediately for 35–40 minutes. Cool thoroughly before serving.

EF; NF; DF

Gluten-free chocolate cake

¾ cup oil
¾ cup cocoa powder, sifted
6 large eggs, separated (at room temperature)
2¼ cups sugar

juice of ½ lemon, strained
1 cup potato flour, sifted twice
¼ tsp salt
icing sugar for decoration

1. Preheat the oven to 180 °C. Grease a medium-sized square cake tin.
2. Whisk the oil into the cocoa powder and set aside.
3. In a separate bowl, beat the egg yolks, sugar, lemon juice and flour, adding the flour a tablespoon at a time. Beat in the cocoa-oil mixture until combined.
4. Separately beat the egg whites and salt just a little beyond the soft-peak stage. Fold the egg whites gently but thoroughly into the cake batter.
5. Pour the batter into the greased tin and bake for 40–50 minutes, until the cake pulls away slightly from the sides or a skewer inserted in the centre comes out clean. Remove from the oven and allow to cool for 10 minutes before inverting gently onto a wire rack. This is a dense, moist cake and does not require icing. Sift over a little icing sugar when cooled for decoration.

GF; WF; NF; DF

Moist chocolate cake

Moist chocolate cake

2¾ cups cake flour
2 cups sugar
⅔ cup cocoa powder
2 tsp bicarbonate of soda
1 tsp salt

2 cups water
⅔ cup sunflower oil
2 tsp vanilla essence
2 tsp vinegar
icing sugar for dusting

1. Preheat the oven to 180 °C. Grease a bundt cake tin.
2. Sift together the dry ingredients and, in a separate bowl, whisk together the wet ingredients. Add the wet ingredients to the dry and mix well. This batter is VERY thin.
3. Pour the batter into the greased cake tin and tap to settle it.
4. Bake for 50–60 minutes until a toothpick inserted in the centre comes out clean. Leave to stand for 5 minutes before carefully inverting onto a wire rack. When completely cooled, slide onto a round platter and sift over some icing sugar.

EF; NF; DF

Chocolate chip & orange biscuits

¾ cup butter or margarine at room temperature
¼ cup icing sugar, sifted
1 cup self-raising flour

½ tsp salt
½–1 tsp grated orange zest (no rind)
60 g plain chocolate chips

1. Mix all of the ingredients, except the chocolate chips, in a bowl until just blended. Sprinkle over the chocolate chips and mix them in.
2. On a lightly floured surface, knead the dough until pliable, form into a ball and cover with clingfilm. Chill in the fridge for 1 hour or until you are ready to bake.
3. Preheat the oven to 180 °C. Roll out the dough onto a lightly floured surface to about 0.5 cm thick. Cut into shapes using a variety of cookie cutters and place on either sheets of ungreased baking paper or baking trays sprayed with non-stick cooking spray.
4. Bake for 10 minutes, keeping a close watch as they burn easily. Remove from the oven and allow to cool.

EF; NF; alt DF | Makes 25–30

Oatmeal & raisin biscuits

Thanks to Chani for this recipe. These freeze well, so double the recipe and freeze a batch.

¾ cup margarine or butter at room temperature
¾ cup white sugar
¾ cup packed brown sugar
2 eggs or 2 tsp Orgran No Egg powder
    mixed with 2 Tbsp water
1 tsp vanilla essence

1¼ cups all-purpose flour or 1 cup rye flour
1 tsp bicarbonate of soda
¾ tsp ground cinnamon
½ tsp salt
2¾ cups rolled oats
1 cup seedless raisins

1. Preheat the oven to 180 °C.
2. In a large bowl, cream the margarine or butter and sugars until smooth. Beat in the eggs or Orgran No Egg blend and the vanilla essence until fluffy.
3. In a separate bowl, combine the flour, bicarbonate of soda, cinnamon and salt. Gradually beat this into the egg mixture. Stir in the oats and raisins. Drop teaspoonfuls of the mixture onto sheets of ungreased baking paper. These spread, so space apart. Bake for 8–10 minutes until golden brown (be careful, they burn easily). Batches waiting to go into the oven can be kept in the fridge.
4. Remove from the oven and cool for 5 minutes, before transferring to a wire rack to cool completely. These biscuits make a delicious dessert derved with a dollop of whipped (non-dairy) cream or ice cream.

NF; alt DF; alt EF; alt WF | Makes 24–30

Chocolate chip
& orange biscuits

Basic biscuits

125 g dairy-free margarine
½ cup white or brown sugar
½ tsp vanilla essence
1 tsp baking powder

1¼ cups flour (combine rice and millet flour or rice and barley flour)
¼ tsp salt
cocoa powder/coconut/dried fruit (optional)

1. Preheat the oven to 170 °C. Spray a baking tray with non-stick cooking spray.
2. Cream the margarine and sugar using a wooden spoon. Add the vanilla essence and mix.
3. Sift in the baking powder, flour and salt, and combine with a wooden spoon. If you'd like, add some cocoa powder, desiccated coconut or chopped dried fruit to the dough.
4. Roll out the dough on a lightly floured surface and shape into balls. Place on the baking tray, spaced apart, and flatten slightly. Bake for 15–20 minutes.

EF; WF; NF; DF; alt GF | Makes 12

Spice biscuits

2 cups cake flour or 1¾ cups bread flour
2 tsp baking powder
2 Tbsp sugar (more if desired)
¼ tsp salt
1 tsp ground ginger
1 tsp ground cinnamon

¼ tsp ground allspice
¼ tsp crushed cloves (optional)
3 Tbsp dairy-free margarine
¾ cup soy/rice/cow's milk
1 tsp vanilla essence
melted dairy-free margarine for brushing

1. Preheat the oven to 190 °C. Spray a baking tray with non-stick cooking spray.
2. Sift together the flour, baking powder, sugar, salt and spices. Cut the margarine into the flour and mix with a wooden spoon.
3. Make a well in the centre and add the milk and vanilla essence. Mix slowly. When blended, stir vigorously until the dough comes away from the sides of the bowl.
4. Turn out onto a lightly floured board and knead gently. Roll to the desired thickness and cut into shapes with cookie cutters. Place onto the baking tray and brush with some melted margarine.
5. Bake for about 12 minutes, or until done.

EF; NF; alt DF | Makes 18–20

TIP: This versatile dough can be used for lining pie crusts. Simply omit all the spices and chill the dough in the fridge for 1 hour. Roll out on a well-floured surface with a rolling pin. Press into a greased quiche or pie dish and blind bake for 5–10 minutes. Then fill the crust with drained pie apples or canned peaches and a little reserved syrup. Sprinkle with cinnamon and return to the oven for a further 20 minutes.

Elisheva's biscuits

This recipe makes a large quantity of biscuits, making it good for a party. The baked biscuits freeze well.

8 cups cake flour
1 tsp salt
500 g dairy-free margarine
2 tsp vanilla essence

2 cups sugar
1 cup smooth apricot jam
4 tsp bicarbonate of soda

1. Preheat the oven to 190 °C.
2. Sift the flour and salt into a bowl and cut in the margarine. Add the vanilla essence and rub together with fingers or use an electric a mixer.
3. In a separate bowl, mix the sugar and jam with a wooden spoon. Mix 1 Tbsp with the bicarbonate of soda, then add this back to the jam mixture and mix well.
4. Add the jam mixture to the flour mixture. Put the combined mixture into a mixer with a dough hook or knead well with floured hands until smooth.
5. On a lightly floured surface, roll out the dough to approximately 5 mm thick and cut out shapes with a cookie cutter. Alternatively, roll into balls and flatten with the back of a fork.
6. Place on either sheets of ungreased baking paper or baking trays sprayed with non-stick cooking spray and bake for 15 minutes, being careful not to burn them. Serve on a platter with icing sugar sifted over.

EF; DF; NF | Makes 130–140

TIP: For variation, add dairy-free chocolate chips to the dough. Or substitute almond essence for the vanilla essence and mix ½ cup flaked almonds into the dough before baking.

Custard biscuits

¾ cup icing sugar, sifted twice
250 g dairy-free margarine
1 tsp vanilla essence
1 tsp baking powder

2 cups flour (combine rice and millet flour or rice and barley flour)
1 cup custard powder

1. Preheat the oven to 180 °C. Spray a baking tray with non-stick cooking spray.
2. Cream the icing sugar and margarine. Add the vanilla essence and baking powder.
3. Add the flour and custard powder and mix to form a dough.
4. Form the dough into small balls, place them on the baking tray and flatten with a fork.
5. Bake for about 20 minuntes, then remove from the oven and allow to cool on the tray. Sift over a little extra icing sugar when cooled.

WF; DF; EF; NF; alt GF | Makes 18–20

Vegan peanut butter cookies

1 cup cake flour
1 tsp baking powder
½ tsp salt
1 cup creamy (smooth) peanut butter

½ cup brown sugar
⅛ cup soy/rice/almond/cow's milk (use more if necessary)
½ cup rolled oats

1. Preheat the oven to 180 °C. Lightly grease a baking tray or line it with baking paper.
2. Combine the flour, baking powder and salt in a large mixing bowl. Set aside.
3. Place the peanut butter into a microwaveable bowl and heat in the microwave for about 45 seconds or until soft. Stir in the sugar and milk, adding enough milk to get a milky consistency. Whisk until smooth.
4. Pour the peanut butter mixture immediately into the bowl containing the dry ingredients. Mix until slightly moist. Add the rolled oats.
5. Continue mixing until well combined. You may have to add more milk, as this batter will be thick. Drop spoonfuls of the batter onto the lined baking tray and bake for approximately 10 minutes. Watch carefully, as these biscuits burn easily.

EF; alt DF | Makes 18

TIP: This recipe can be easily doubled and the biscuits freeze well.

No-bake chocolate clusters

2 cups dark cooking chocolate
1 cup seedless raisins

1 cup cornflakes (optional)

1. Break the chocolate into a glass bowl. Boil a medium-sized pot of water, place the bowl over the water and cover the chocolate with the lid of the pot. Alternatively, use a double boiler to melt the chocolate. Make sure that no water gets into the chocolate.
2. When the chocolate has melted, stir in the raisins first and then the cornflakes (if using).
3. Cover 2 baking trays with baking paper or grease lightly. Drop spoonfuls of the mixture onto the trays, leaving spaces in-between. Place in the fridge to set.
4. Serve alone or with Coffee 'Ice Cream' (see page 77). Store the clusters in an airtight container in a cool dark place. They also freeze well.

DF; WF; NF; EF; alt GF | Makes 18–20

TIP: Some cornflakes contain barley malt, which contains gluten. If gluten intolerant, leave out the cornflakes and just use raisins..

Raspberry squares

Raspberry squares

1¼ cups sifted cake/rice flour
1¼ cups quick rolled oats
1 cup melted dairy-free margarine

1 cup brown sugar
a pinch of salt
¾–1 cup raspberry jam

1. Preheat the oven to 180 °C. Grease a small baking tray or casserole dish.
2. Combine all of the ingredients, except the jam.
3. Press half of the mixture onto the greased baking tray or dish and spread over the jam.
4. Cover the jam with the rest of the mixture and smooth over.
5. Bake for 30 minutes.
6. Cut into squares while warm and leave in the tray to cool.

EF; DF; alt WF | Makes 18

TIP: Use strawberry or apricot instead of raspberry jam for variation.

The classic crunchie

The classic crunchie

4 cups oats
2 cups cake flour or 1 cup rye flour
2 cups desiccated coconut
2 Tbsp sesame seeds (optional)

250 g dairy-free margarine
3 Tbsp Golden syrup (optional)
2 cups sugar
1 level tsp bicarbonate of soda

1. Preheat the oven to 180 °C. Line a baking tray with baking paper and grease.
2. In a large bowl, mix the oats, flour, coconut and sesame seeds (if using).
3. Heat the margarine and syrup (if using) with the sugar in a saucepan, stirring regularly until the sugar melts and starts to bubble. Caution: sugar burns easily, so keep a close watch. Remove from the heat and add the bicarbonate of soda (the mixture will foam and thicken a bit).
4. Immediately make a well in the centre of the dry ingredients and pour in the hot mixture. Mix well.
5. Leave to cool for a few minutes. When cool enough to handle, press the mixture into the lined baking tray and bake on the top shelf of the oven for 12–15 minutes. Remove from the oven and cut into rectangles while hot, then leave to cool in the tray.

DF; EF; alt WF | Makes 24–30

TIP: For a fancier version, melt 1 cup non-dairy chocolate pieces with 2 Tbsp soy milk in a small saucepan over a low heat. Either dip the individual cooled crunchies halfway into the chocolate sauce or drizzle it over them. Place on a sheet of greaseproof paper to cool.

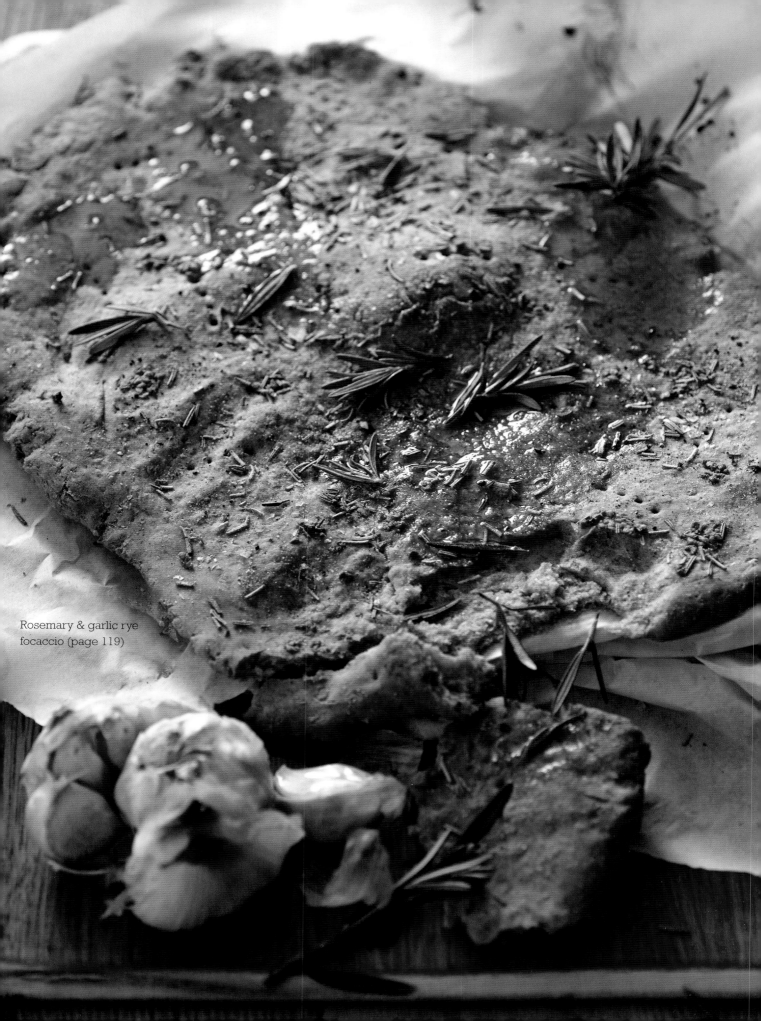

Rosemary & garlic rye
focaccio (page 119)

Bread is the king of the table and all else is merely the court that surrounds the king. The countries are the soup, the meat, the vegetables, the salad, but bread is king.

Louis Bromfield

Breads

Bread is a staple in all of our lives and in our daily diet. Most people visit their 'regular' supermarket to buy 'regular' bread. When I got to Seattle and saw the variety of alternative breads stocked in the health-food supermarkets I was stunned. South Africans are starting to become more aware and you can find a delicious 'safe' loaf in most health-food shops today. This requires a detour though and is often prohibitively expensive on an ongoing basis. I keep a stock of flours and, most often, make my own bread. Sandwiches for work and school lunches are generally made using the 100% rye bread (see page 106) or Tammi's water challah (see page 110). Keep a loaf or two presliced in the freezer and take out for toasting as needed. I also keep a stock of sweet potato mini muffin breads (see page 118) in the freezer. They're good for picnic lunches or snacks.

Gluten-free flour blends

To make gluten-free flour that works, you can combine two or three of the flours below in equal parts. These flours work best in combination as they don't contain the 'glue'-ten to stick them together. Some of them have strong tastes, such as chickpea and soya flour, and are best used with sorghum meal, maize meal or rice flour. As they do not bind well, the recipes should be a little more 'wet' in consistency. An egg or Orgran No Egg egg substitute works well as a binder. Instead of or in addition to an egg, one teaspoon xanthan gum also works as a good binder. I most often use a combination of yellow maize flour, rice flour and/or sorghum meal.

sorghum meal	flax meal
chickpea flour	rice and brown rice flours
potato flour	millet flour
tapioca flour	quinoa flour
yellow or white maize (corn) meal or flour	oat flour (Note that not all coeliacs include
soya flour	oats in their diets.)
almond meal	

TIP: Maltabella is sorghum meal. Use as is in your bread – it's delicious!

100% rye bread

This quick and easy rye bread tastes good and freezes well. It's very heavy in texture, so slice thinly.

2 x 10 g sachets instant dry yeast
½ cup sugar or fructose
1½–2 cups warm water

½ cup oil
1 tsp salt
1 kg rye flour (fine is best)

1. Preheat the oven to 180 °C. Grease a baking tray with oil.
2. Place the yeast, sugar or fructose and water in a large, shallow bowl or mixer. Leave for 5–10 minutes until foamy (allowing the yeast to prove).
3. Add the oil and salt, and stir. Add the flour, 1 cup at a time, stirring until it all 'sticks' together.
4. Dust your hands with flour and knead the dough. Divide it in half and form each into a roughly round shape. Place them on the baking tray and rub the tops with a little water. Leave to rise for 30–45 minutes.
5. Bake on the middle shelf of the oven for 1 hour. The crusts will be crispy and brown. Enjoy plain or toasted with jam.

WF; DF; EF; NF | Makes 2 loaves

100% rye bread

Corn, rice
& soya bread

Corn, rice & soya bread

4 cups yellow maize meal or polenta	1 x 410 g can creamstyle sweetcorn
3 cups brown or white rice flour	1½ cups warm water
1 cup soya/sorghum/millet flour	1 cup soy milk
8 tsp baking powder	½ cup oil
¼ cup fructose	2 eggs or 2 tsp Orgran No Egg powder
1 Tbsp herb and garlic salt	mixed with 2 Tbsp hot water

1. Preheat the oven to 180 °C. Grease 2 loaf tins or 2 muffin pans.
2. Place the maize meal or polenta, flours, baking powder, fructose and salt in a large, shallow bowl or mixer.
3. In a separate bowl, whisk the sweetcorn, water, soy milk, oil and eggs or egg substitute until blended.
4. Make a well in the centre of the dry ingredients and pour in the sweetcorn mixture. Mix until just blended. You may need to add more water to create a dropping consistency. Pour into the loaf tins or muffin pans.
5. Sprinkle with extra herb and garlic salt and bake for 40–50 minutes until the bread pulls away from the sides of the tin or pan. Serve with sundried tomato pesto, olives and hummus for a nutritious meal.

WF; GF; DF; NF; alt EF | Makes 2 loaves or 18 muffins

Pronutro bread

This bread is slightly sweet. Although still crumbly, it is less so than most gluten-free breads.

1 cup original wheat-free Pronutro	3 Tbsp baking powder
1 cup sorghum meal or uncooked Maltabella	1 tsp salt
½ cup maize meal	½ cup sunflower oil
½ cup sunflower seeds ground into meal	3 extra-large eggs
½ cup pumpkin seeds ground into meal	1 cup soy milk
½ cup soya flour or sesame seeds	1 cup warm water
½ cup brown sugar	

1. Preheat the oven to 160 °C. Spray a loaf tin with non-stick cooking spray.
2. Combine all of the dry ingredients in a large mixing bowl and whisk well.
3. In a separate bowl, whisk the oil and eggs, add the soy milk and whisk again. Finally, whisk in the water.
4. Make a well in the centre of the dry ingredients and pour in the wet mixture. Mix until just blended. The consistency should be that of wet porridge. You may need to add a little extra water.
5. Pour into the loaf tin and bake immediately for about 1 hour or until a skewer inserted into the centre comes out clean. Switch off the oven, open the door a little and leave the loaf in for 10 minutes. Remove from the oven and leave to stand for 10 minutes before carefully turning out onto a rack to cool.

WF; GF; DF; NF | Makes 1 loaf

Tammi's water challah

Challah is a traditional Jewish bread eaten on the Sabbath and holidays. I learned to make this dense and delicious challah in Seattle. Americans call it 'water challah', as challah is usually made using egg, whereas here extra water is substituted. The dining table is compared to an altar and challah to the sacrifice. It's so good it's like manna. It's always eaten up to the last crumb. I highly recommend a slice with soup.

This bulk recipe makes six loaves. Freeze the extras when cooled in plastic freezer bags and defrost as needed. Just before serving, warm a loaf in the oven wrapped in foil. It will taste freshly baked.

3 x 10 g sachets active dry yeast
1½ cups sugar (if you want, you can substitute some of the sugar with honey)
6 cups warm water (not hot)

1½ cups sunflower or olive oil
2 Tbsp salt
1 x 2.5 kg pkt bread flour

1. Place the yeast and sugar in a large, round, flat-bottomed bowl and cover with the water. Leave for 5–7 minutes to allow the yeast to prove.
2. Add the oil and salt, and stir.
3. Add the flour, a quarter of the packet at a time, reserving ½ cup for dusting your hands and work surface. Start by mixing with a wooden spoon until a ball of dough forms. Then dust your hands with the reserved flour and knead the dough for 10–15 minutes. To knead the dough, push it away from you with the heel of your hand, then pick up the front of the dough with your fingers and pull it back towards your body as if you are folding it in half. Then repeat, pushing it away from you with the heel of your hand, until it becomes difficult to knead. Once this happens, allow the dough to rest for a few minutes; the dough will 'relax' and you can then knead it again until it is smooth and elastic. The purpose of kneading is to stretch out the gluten strands in the flour so that they stick together better, and trap the air bubbles created by the yeast, which gives you a lighter, fluffier bread.
4. Put the dough into the bowl and cover it with a damp dish cloth or towel and leave in a warm place to rise for about 45 minutes, until the dough has doubled in size. On a cold day, the dough will take much longer to rise.
5. When ready to bake, preheat the oven to 180 °C. Oil or lightly dust a baking tray with flour.
6. Once risen, punch down the dough in the bowl, turn it out onto a lightly floured surface and knead again.
7. Using a bread knife, divide the dough by cutting it in half and then into thirds – making 6 equal-sized pieces. Then divide each piece again into 3 or 4. Roll each small piece into a 'snake' and braid. Don't forget to tuck the ends under. Place onto the prepared baking tray.
8. When you have braided all 6 loaves, use a clean paint brush or pastry brush to brush each loaf with a little water and leave to rise for 10–15 minutes.
9. Bake for 30–35 minutes until the tops are lightly browned.

EF; DF; NF | Makes 6 loaves

TIP: I keep an empty spice container filled with flour handy for sprinkling surfaces or my hands with extra flour as needed. A spray bottle filled with water is also a useful tool. I use it to mist the inside of the oven before baking. This ensures an even-baked crust. Another empty spice bottle can be filled with equal amounts of cinnamon and sugar to sprinkle onto challah before baking.

Tammi's water challah

[Breadbaking is] one of those almost hypnotic businesses, like a dance from some ancient ceremony. It leaves you filled with one of the world's sweetest smells ... there is no chiropractic treatment, no yoga exercise, no hour of meditation in a music-throbbing chapel that will leave you emptier of bad thoughts than this homely ceremony of making bread.

M.F.K. Fisher, *The Art of Eating*

Challah knot rolls

1 x 10 g sachet active dry yeast
½ cup sugar
1½–2 cups warm water (not hot)

½ cup sunflower or olive oil
1 tsp salt
6 cups bread flour

1. Repeat Steps 1–6 of the recipe on page 110.
2. Divide the dough into 12 equal-sized pieces and roll each piece into a 'snake'. Tie each snake in a knot and tuck the ends under. Place on the greased baking tray and bake for 25–30 minutes.

EF; DF; NF | Makes 12 rolls

TIP: Drizzle some honey or sprinkle some cinnamon sugar on top of the rolls before baking.

Orange walnut bread

2 cups gluten-free flour blend (see below) or rye/wholewheat flour
¾ cup sugar
½ cup coconut/soy milk
½ cup orange juice
2 Tbsp melted butter or oil

4 Tbsp apple sauce plus 1 Tbsp coconut/soy milk
2 Tbsp freshly grated orange zest
1½ tsp baking powder
½ tsp salt
¾ cup chopped walnuts

1. Preheat the oven to 180 °C. Grease a medium-sized loaf tin.
2. Combine all of the ingredients, except the walnuts, in a large bowl and beat at medium speed until well mixed. Stir in the walnuts.
3. Pour into the loaf tin and bake for 50–60 minutes or until a toothpick inserted in the centre comes out clean. Allow to cool for 10 minutes before removing from the tin.

EF; alt WF; alt GF; alt DF | Makes 1 loaf

FLOUR BLEND: Combine 2 cups rice flour, ⅔ cup potato starch, ⅓ cup tapioca flour and 1 tsp xanthan gum (available from health shops). Use the appropriate amount for this recipe and store the remainder in an airtight container.

Half wholewheat challah

This is a 'healthier' version of the traditional plaited Jewish challah. The dough shapes and handles the same way and it is delicious when baked. It's an especially tasty treat when cut into slices, toasted and served spread with a bit of butter and sprinkled with cinnamon sugar.

1 x 10 g sachet active dry yeast
½ cup brown sugar
1⅔ cups warm water (not hot)
½ cup sunflower oil

1–2 tsp salt
3 cups wholewheat flour
2½ cups white bread flour

1. Place the yeast and sugar in a large, round, flat-bottomed bowl and cover with the water. Leave for 5–7 minutes to allow the yeast to prove. Add the oil and salt.
2. Add the flours, 2 cups at a time, mixing with a wooden spoon until a sticky ball of dough forms.
3. Dust your hands with flour and knead the dough for 10–15 minutes. Pour a teaspoon of oil into your hands and rub onto the ball of dough. Place in the bowl and cover with a damp dish cloth or towel and leave to rise in a warm place for about 45 minutes until it has doubled in size.
4. Once risen, punch down the dough in the bowl, turn out onto a lightly floured surface and knead again a few times.
5. Preheat the oven to 180 °C. Line 2 baking trays with baking paper or lightly dust with flour.
6. Divide the dough in half and then into thirds, so that you have 6 equal-sized pieces. Roll the pieces into 'snakes' of equal length, 25–30 cm long. Pinch the ends of 3 snakes together and plait the strands, pinching the ends together. Tuck both ends under and place on the prepared baking tray. Repeat with the other half.
7. Wet your fingers and very lightly wet the tops of the loaves with water. Alternatively, you can lightly brush them with beaten egg. Let the loaves stand for 5–10 minutes.
8. Bake for 25–35 minutes until well risen and browned on top. Remove from the oven and allow to cool for 5 minutes, then place on a wire rack. This step is to prevent the very hot steam-filled loaf from becoming soggy at the bottom.

EF; DF | Makes 2 loaves

TIP: Sprinkle the top of the loaves with cinnamon sugar before baking. If doing so, they must be baked on lined or well-greased baking trays or the loaves will stick to the tray.

Rye & oat mini muffin breads

1½–2 cups warm water
½ cup brown or white sugar
2 x 10 g sachets instant dry yeast
1 cup breakfast oats

½ cup oat bran
¼ cup olive oil
1 Tbsp salt
1 kg rye flour

1. Place 1½ cups water and the sugar in a large, shallow bowl. Sprinkle over the yeast and leave to prove for 5 minutes. Then sprinkle over the oats and oat bran, and leave for a further 5 minutes.
2. Add the oil and salt, followed by the rye flour, 1 cup at a time. Reserve 2 Tbsp flour for dusting your hands and work surface. You may need to add the extra ½ cup water; if so, add it ¼ cup at a time, alternating with the flour. Mix with a large spoon. The dough will be quite stiff, but not too stiff.
3. Dust your hands with some of the reserved flour and knead the dough lightly.
4. Place a teacup half-filled with cold water into the oven and preheat to 180 °C. Grease a muffin pan or mini loaf tins well. Divide the dough into 12 portions. Roll each between your floured palms and place into the muffin pan or tins. Leave to rise for 45 minutes (60 minutes if it's a very cold day). Sprinkle some oats on top of each before baking.
5. Leaving the teacup in the oven (to steam the inside), place the muffin pan or tins on the middle shelf and bake for 45 minutes. Then switch off the oven and leave the breads inside for a further 10 minutes.
6. These are great for school and office lunches, with spreads or with jam and cheese.

WF; EF; DF | Makes 12

Fruity rye, oat & corn bread

3 cups yellow or white maize meal
2 cups rye flour
2 Tbsp baking powder
1 tsp salt
1 cup raw Jungle Oats
½ cup sugar or ⅔ cup fructose

¾ cup seedless raisins
½ cup sunflower seeds (optional)
½ cup sunflower oil
2 cups warm water
1 cup grated apple or mashed banana
cinnamon sugar for sprinkling

1. Preheat the oven to 180 °C. Grease or line 2 loaf tins.
2. Combine all of the dry ingredients, including the raisins and seeds (if using). Make a well in the centre and pour in the oil and water. Add the apple or banana and mix until just blended. The mixture will be quite lumpy and sticky.
3. Spoon into the loaf tins and sprinkle a few drops of water on top. Sprinkle over a little cinnamon sugar and bake for 1 hour or until the loaves pull away from the sides of the tins. Switch off the oven and leave the loaves in for a few more minutes to crisp before turning out onto a rack to cool.
4. Cut thick slices and top with a drizzle of honey, a lick of peanut butter or some cheese, or just eat plain.

YF; WF; DF; NF; alt SF | Makes 2 loaves

Rye & oat
mini muffin breads

Wheat-free seed loaf

3 cups yellow or white maize meal
2 cups rye flour
2 Tbsp baking powder
1 Tbsp salt
1 cup raw Jungle Oats
½ cup sugar or fructose
½ cup sunflower seeds

¼ cup pumpkin seeds
¼ cup sesame seeds
¼ cup linseeds/flax seeds
¾ cup seedless raisins (optional)
½ cup sunflower oil
2 cups warm water

1. Preheat the oven to 180 °C. Grease 2 loaf tins.
2. Combine all of the dry ingredients, including the seeds and raisins (if using). Make a well in the centre and pour in the oil and water. Mix until just blended. The mixture will be quite lumpy and sticky.
3. Spoon into the loaf tins and sprinkle a few drops of water on top.
4. Bake for 1 hour or until the loaves have pulled away from the sides of the tins. Switch off the oven and leave the loaves in for a few minutes to crisp before turning out onto a rack to cool. Cut into thick slices only when cool. This bread is dense, crumbly and delicious.

WF; EF; NF; DF; YF | Makes 2 loaves

Dilly beer bread

3 cups white bread flour
1 tsp salt
2 tsp baking powder

2 Tbsp brown sugar
2 Tbsp chopped fresh dill or 1 Tbsp dried
1 x 340 ml can beer

1. Preheat the oven to 160 °C. Grease a small loaf tin well.
2. Sift together the flour, salt and baking powder. Add the sugar and dill, and mix thoroughly.
3. Make a well in the centre and pour in the beer. Mix to combine and then knead lightly to form a stiff dough. Place in the loaf tin and bake for 1 hour or until browned on top and pulling away from the sides. A skewer inserted in the centre should come out clean. Turn out onto a wire rack to cool before serving.

EF; DF; NF | Makes 1 small loaf

The smell of good bread baking, like the sound of lightly flowing water, is indescribable in its evocation of innocence and delight...

M.F.K. Fisher, *The Art of Eating*

Self-raising flour corn bread

This bread is perfect at a braai.

2 cups self-raising flour	1 Tbsp sugar
1 tsp baking powder	1 egg
½ tsp salt	1 x 410 g can creamstyle sweetcorn

1. Preheat the oven to 180 °C. Grease a loaf tin.
2. Sift the flour, baking powder and salt into a bowl and stir in the sugar.
3. In a separate bowl, whisk the egg and add the sweetcorn. Add this to the dry ingredients and mix until just blended. Spoon into the loaf tin and bake for 1 hour. Turn out onto a wire rack to cool.

DF; YF; NF | Makes 1 loaf

Onion bagel sticks

1 x 10 g sachet instant dry yeast	1½ tsp salt
2 tsp sugar	½ cup matzo meal or oat bran
1½ cups warm water (not hot)	1 large onion, peeled and diced
¼ cup olive oil	2 tsp paprika
3½ cups bread flour + extra ½ cup	2 tsp dried granulated garlic

1. Dissolve the yeast and sugar in the warm water. Add half of the olive oil, 2 cups of the flour and 1 tsp of the salt, and mix. Continue to add the remaining 1½ cups flour, alternating with the matzo meal or oat bran, until all have been added. Mix until the dough is stiff, but not hard.
2. Knead the dough on a lightly floured surface for 5 minutes. Place in a large, greased plastic bowl and turn it over once so that all sides are lightly greased. Cover the bowl with a damp dish cloth and allow the dough to rise for about 1 hour until doubled in size. When risen, punch down several times, sprinkle over the extra ½ cup flour and knead it in. Allow to rest for 5 minutes.
3. Preheat the oven to 180 °C. Grease a baking tray.
4. Cut the dough into 8 pieces and roll each into a fat stick, about 15 cm long. Place on the baking tray and slightly flatten each with the heel of your hand. Brush the tops with the remaining olive oil and sprinkle each generously with the diced onion. Press the onions gently into the dough with your fingertips and sprinkle over the rest of the salt, the paprika and garlic. Bake until the bagel sticks are light golden brown and crispy on the top and bottom, 15–20 minutes. Serve straight out of the oven with soup or salad, or cool and store in an airtight container for up to 3 days.

EF; DF; NF | Makes 8

Savoury bread sticks

1 x 10 g sachet instant dry yeast
2 tsp sugar
1½ cups warm water (not hot)
¼ cup olive oil
3½ cups bread flour
1 tsp herb salt

2½ cups wholewheat or Nutty Wheat flour
1 Tbsp kosher salt
freshly ground black pepper to taste
2 tsp paprika or cayenne pepper
2 tsp dried granulated garlic

1. Dissolve the yeast and sugar in the warm water. Add half of the oil, 2 cups of the bread flour and the herb salt, and start to mix. Continue to mix in the rest of the bread flour, alternating with the wholewheat or Nutty Wheat flour, until all have been added. Mix until the dough is stiff, but not hard.
2. Knead the dough on a lightly floured surface for 5 minutes. Place into a large, greased plastic bowl and turn it over once so that all sides of the dough are lightly greased. Cover the bowl with a damp dish cloth and allow the dough to rise for about 1 hour until doubled in size. When risen, punch down several times and let it rest for 5 minutes.
3. Preheat the oven to 180 °C. Grease a baking tray.
4. Cut the dough into 12 pieces and roll each into a thin 'snake', 15–20 cm long. Place on the baking tray and brush the tops with the remaining oil. Sprinkle each generously with the kosher salt and press down gently with your fingertips. Sprinkle over the black pepper, paprika or cayenne pepper and garlic.
5. Bake for 15–20 minutes until light golden brown and crispy on the top and bottom. Watch them, as they burn easily. Serve warm straight out of the oven, or cool and store in an airtight container for up to 3 days.

DF; EF; NF | Makes 12

Sweet potato bread

This batter bread is versatile and delicious. Bake it in muffin pans to make mini muffin breads.

1 large sweet potato, cooked until soft, skin
    removed and roughly chopped
1 cup rice flour
1 cup finely ground yellow polenta meal

1 cup soy milk
2 Tbsp sunflower oil
1 heaped tsp baking powder
½ tsp salt or herb salt

1. Preheat the oven to 180 °C. Oil a small loaf tin.
2. Place all of the ingredients into a food processor and, using the blade attachment, whizz until smooth.
3. Transfer the batter to the loaf tin and bake for 40 minutes or until beginning to brown on top.

WF; GF; DF; YF; SF | Makes 1 small loaf

Rosemary & garlic rye focaccia

1 x 10 g sachet instant dry yeast
1 tsp sugar
1 cup warm water (not hot)
¼ cup extra-virgin olive oil
1 Tbsp fresh chopped rosemary
½ tsp crushed garlic

1 tsp salt
500 g rye flour (stoneground or fine)
¼ cup maize meal or extra rye flour
extra olive oil for drizzling
extra rosemary for sprinkling
salt and freshly ground black pepper to taste

1. Place the yeast and sugar in a large, round, flat-bottomed bowl and cover with the water. Leave for 5–7 minutes to allow the yeast to prove, then add the oil (reserving 1 Tbsp), rosemary, garlic and salt.
2. Add the flour, 2 cups at a time, mixing with a wooden spoon until a sticky ball of dough forms. Rub the dough with the reserved oil, then cover the bowl with a damp dish cloth and leave to rise for 1 hour. Rye flour is heavy and has little gluten so it will not rise as much as wheat flour.
3. Preheat the oven to 180 °C. Grease 2 baking trays.
4. When the dough has risen, sprinkle over the maize meal or extra rye flour and punch down. The dough will remain sticky. Halve the dough and, on a floured surface, roll each half into a ball. Place on the baking trays and press into discs about 2.5 cm thick. Drizzle the discs with olive oil, sprinkle with extra rosemary and season with salt and black pepper. Prick a few times with a fork.
5. Bake for 30–40 minutes and serve hot, straight from the oven, cut into pie-shaped wedges.

WF; DF; EF; NF | Makes 2

Wholewheat bread

Also known as 'candida bread' as people who suffer from candida must not have yeast. If you have candida, omit the sugar and use sweetener instead.

3 cups wholewheat flour
1 tsp baking powder
1 tsp bicarbonate of soda
¼ cup rolled oats

½ tsp salt
1 Tbsp sugar or xylitol or stevia
1½ Tbsp soft butter or 2 Tbsp canola oil
2 cups rice/soy/buttermilk

1. Preheat the oven to 200 °C. Grease a loaf tin.
2. Combine all of the dry ingredients, then mix in the butter or oil with a fork.
3. Add the milk (and sweetener if it is a liquid) and mix until well combined.
4. Put the mixture into the loaf tin and bake for 50 minutes. Turn out onto a wire rack to cool.

YF; EF; alt DF; alt SF | Makes 1 loaf

Rustic sundried tomato & basil bread

Rustic sundried tomato & basil bread

½ cup sundried tomatoes
1 cup hot rooibos tea
1 x 10 g sachet active dry yeast
2 Tbsp brown sugar
2 cups warm water (not hot)
¼ cup olive oil

1–2 tsp salt
freshly ground black pepper to taste
3½ cups wholewheat flour
2 cups white bread flour
½ cup fresh basil leaves
extra olive oil for rubbing

1. Place the sundried tomatoes into a bowl with the rooibos tea and set aside.
2. Place the yeast and sugar in a large, round, flat-bottomed bowl and cover with the water. Leave for 5–7 minutes to to prove, then add the oil, salt and a few twists of ground black pepper.
3. Add the flours, 2 cups at a time, mixing with a wooden spoon until a sticky ball of dough forms.
4. Reserving 5 or 6 leaves for decoration, tear the basil into large pieces and sprinkle these over the dough. Drain the sundried tomatoes in a sieve and, reserving 5 or 6 for decoration, sprinkle over the dough and press in with your index finger. Dust your hands with flour and knead the basil and sundried tomatoes into the dough. Pour a teaspoon of oil into your hands and rub onto the ball of dough. Place the dough in the bowl, cover with a damp dish cloth or towel and leave to rise in a warm place until the dough has doubled in size.
5. Preheat the oven to 180 °C. Sprinkle 2 baking trays with flour or maize meal.
6. Punch down the dough in the bowl, turn it out onto a lightly floured surface and knead again a few times.
7. Divide the dough in half and shape each into an oval. Place the loaves onto the prepared baking trays. Rub with olive oil and lightly press the reserved basil and sundried tomatoes into the top of each. Grind over a little extra black pepper and leave the loaves to stand for 10 minutes.
8. Mist the inside of the oven with water and allow it to reach the correct temperature again. Bake the loaves for 45–50 minutes until browned on top. Remove from the oven and allow to cool on a wire rack. These freeze well; allow to cool completely before freezing.

`EF; DF; NF | Makes 2`

TIP: This is delicious dipped in olive oil or spread with butter.

Good bread is the great need in poor homes, and oftentimes the best appreciated luxury in the homes of the very rich.

The Pillsbury Company, *A Book for a Cook*

Rye & sorghum yeast bread

1 x 10 g sachet instant dry yeast	1 tsp salt
1 Tbsp sugar	2 cups rye flour, sifted
2 cups warm water (not hot)	3 cups sorghum flour/meal
2 Tbsp sunflower oil	

1. Dissolve the yeast and sugar in the water in a medium-sized bowl. Leave to prove for 5–10 minutes.
2. Add the oil, salt and rye flour, and stir well. Add the sorghum flour/meal and stir until blended. The mixture will be dark brown and very sticky and wet.
3. Spoon the mixture into 2 well-oiled or lined loaf tins and smooth the tops with the back of a wet spoon. Leave to rise in a warm place for 1–2 hours. The breads will be ready to bake when they have risen almost to the top of the loaf tins – they will look bubbly and grainy.
4. When nearly there, preheat the oven to 180 °C.
5. Bake for 50 minutes. Remove from the oven and allow to stand for 10 minutes before turning out onto a wire rack to cool. This recipe can also be made in muffin pans.

WF; DF; EF; NF | Makes 2 loaves

Onion & herb loaf

1 level tsp mustard	1 tsp dried parsley
1 cup warm water	¼ tsp dried thyme
1 egg or extra 2 Tbsp warm water	½ tsp dried sage
2 cups maize/polenta meal	4 tsp baking powder
½ cup rice flour	1 Tbsp olive oil
1 cup soya flour	1 Tbsp minced onion

1. Preheat the oven to 200 °C. Grease a small loaf tin.
2. If using a food processor, place all of the ingredients in the bowl and process until smooth and well mixed. If mixing by hand, place the mustard in a large bowl and beat with a little water until smooth. Add the remaining ingredients and beat well with a wooden spoon.
3. Place the mixture into the loaf tin and bake in the middle of the oven for about 40 minutes until brown and firm to the touch. Remove from the tin and cool on a wire rack. Store in the fridge in an airtight container and eat within 3 days. This recipe doubles and freezes well.

YF; WF; GF; DF; SF; alt EF | Makes 1 small loaf

Maize meal bread

Maize meal bread

2 cups yellow or white maize meal	½ tsp salt or herb salt
1 egg or 1 tsp Orgran No Egg powder mixed with 1 Tbsp hot water	1½–2 cups soy/goat's/cow's milk
2 tsp bicarbonate of soda	3 Tbsp olive oil

1. Preheat the oven to 180 °C. Line a loaf tin or mini tins with baking paper or spray with non-stick cooking spray.
2. Place all of the ingredients into a blender or food processor and blend well. Alternatively, blend by hand with a wooden spoon. Pour into the prepared tin or mini tins.
3. Bake for 25–30 minutes (20 minutes if making mini loaves) or until golden brown. Turn out carefully onto a wire rack to cool. Slice with a sharp non-serrated knife as this bread is very crumbly.

GF; WF; YF; NF; alt DF; alt EF | Makes 1 loaf

TIP: Millet flour or brown rice flour can be substituted for the maize meal.

Butter bean dip with rye chips (page 126)

Snacks

A snack is a small portion of food as contrasted with a regular meal. Healthy snacks help to keep our blood sugar stable and fuel our engines. With the spread of convenience stores, packaged snack foods are now a significant business. Snack foods are typically designed to be portable, quick and satisfying. Processed snack foods are designed to be less perishable and more appealing than prepared foods. They often contain substantial amounts of sweeteners, preservatives, colourants and flavourings, but contain little nutritional value and lots of allergens!

This chapter contains snack foods that are delicious and healthy. Most DO take a bit of time to make, but then they can be stored in sealed containers or frozen and used as needed. I find it's good to be prepared, so make sure you keep a stock of these healthy 'convenience' foods for school and work lunch boxes, outings, etc.

American-style giant sweet pretzels

1 x 10 g sachet active dry yeast
¾ cup sugar
1 cup warm water
½ cup sunflower oil
½ tsp salt

1 tsp vanilla essence
½ cup apple juice
1 kg bread flour
¼ cup ground cinnamon mixed with
    ½ cup sugar

1. Preheat the oven to 180 °C. Grease 2 or 3 baking trays well. Place the yeast and sugar in a large mixing bowl and stir. Add the warm water and leave for 5 minutes to activate the yeast.
2. When the yeast is bubbly, add the oil, salt, vanilla essence and apple juice. Stir in the flour, 1 cup at a time, until a dough forms. Eventually the dough will become too sticky and you will need to knead the last few cups of flour in with your hands. Knead well and return to the bowl. Cover the bowl with a damp cloth and allow the dough to rise for about 1 hour, until it has doubled in size.
3. When the dough has risen, punch it down and knead again. Divide it into 12–18 pieces and roll each into long, thin 'snakes'. Roll each in the cinnamon sugar and then shape into large pretzels or any other shape you prefer. Place on the greased baking trays and bake for 15 minutes or until lightly browned. Remove from the oven and allow to cool. They last for up to a week stored in airtight containers.

DF; EF; NF | Makes 12–18

Butter bean dip with rye chips

Cans of butter beans are a grocery-cupboard staple. A healthy, low-fat protein, they are good in salads or as a dip or side dish. If time is short, you can substitute store-bought corn chips or nachos for the rye chips.

2 x 410 g cans butter beans
2 cloves garlic
2 Tbsp fresh lemon juice
⅓ cup olive oil + extra 4 Tbsp for drizzling

¼ cup loosely packed flat-leaf fresh parsley
salt and freshly ground black pepper to taste
6 thin slices rye bread, cut into wedges
1 tsp dried origanum

1. Preheat the oven to 200 °C.
2. Place the beans, garlic, lemon juice, oil and parsley in the bowl of a food processor and pulse until the mixture is coarsely chopped. Season to taste and transfer the bean purée to a small bowl.
3. Arrange the rye bread wedges on a large baking tray. Drizzle over the extra oil, then toss and spread out the wedges evenly. Season with the origanum, and some salt and pepper. Bake for 8–12 minutes or until toasted and golden. Serve warm or at room temperature with the bean purée.

DF; EF; NF; WF; SF | Serves 10–12 as a starter

Honey & soy seed mix

This is delicious on its own or as a garnish on salads.

2 Tbsp honey	½ cup sesame seeds
2 Tbsp regular or tamari soy sauce	½ cup pumpkin seeds
½ cup sunflower seeds	1 cup linseeds/flax seeds

1. Heat the oven to 160 °C. Line a baking tray with baking paper or spray with non-stick cooking spray.
2. Warm the honey and mix with the soy sauce.
3. Combine the seeds in a bowl and add the honey-soy. Mix well and spread onto the prepared baking tray. Roast for 1 minute, then remove from the oven, shake the tray and return to the oven for a further 1 minute, no more. Seeds burn very easily.

DF; EF; NF; alt WF; alt GF | Serves 4

TIP: If not allergic to nuts, add ½ cup flaked almonds to the mix before roasting.

Goji berry honey crunch

1 cup pumpkin seeds	2–3 Tbsp honey
½ cup sunflower seeds	½ cup dried goji berries
1 cup flaked almonds (optional)	½ cup dried pomegranate arils (seeds)

1. Preheat the oven to 180 °C. Line a baking tray with baking paper.
2. Mix the seeds and almonds (if using). Spread onto the lined baking tray and drizzle over the honey.
3. Roast for 1 minute, then remove from the oven, shake the tray and return to the oven for a further 1 minute. Remove from the oven and allow to cool before mixing with the goji berries and pomegranate arils. Store in an airtight container.

DF; EF; WF; GF; alt NF | Serves 4–6

TIP: Pomegranate arils are available from health-food stores. If you are unable to source them, they can be substituted with ¼ cup seedless raisins.

Savoury millet 'cakes'

I adapted this recipe from one by Vyvyan Hirshovitz.

2 cups millet
7 cups water
¼ cup sesame seeds

1 Tbsp sunflower oil
1 tsp Herbamare® Herb Seasoning Salt
extra sesame seeds and salt for sprinkling

1. Preheat the oven to 180 °C. Grease a muffin pan.
2. Cook the millet according to the packet instructions, but use 7 cups water.
3. When all the water has cooked away (be careful not to burn), mix in the sesame seeds, oil and seasoning salt. Spoon the mixture into the muffin pan and press down with the back of a spoon to compact. Sprinkle with extra sesame seeds and salt and bake for 20–25 minutes or until the cakes pull away from the sides of the pan.
4. Serve warm or at room temperature, plain or with soup, hummus, cheese or any savoury topping.

DF; EF; NF; WF; GF; SF | Makes 12

Almond polenta 'muffins'

3 cups water
1 cup polenta
1 Tbsp sunflower oil
a pinch of salt

½ cup dark brown sugar
½ cup slivered almonds
ground cinnamon for sprinkling
extra oil for drizzling

1. Preheat the oven to 180 °C. Spray a muffin pan with non-stick cooking spray.
2. Bring the water to the boil in a pot and add the polenta, oil, salt and half of the sugar. Stir until it thickens to a porridge-like consistency.
3. Sprinkle a teaspoon of almonds into the base of each muffin hole and ladle the polenta on top. Press another teaspoon of almonds into the top of each and sprinkle each muffin with a teaspoon of sugar. Sprinkle with the cinnamon and drizzle over a little oil. Leave to cool to allow the polenta to 'set'.
4. Bake for 30–40 minutes until the muffins pull away from the sides of the pan. Remove from the oven and leave to stand for 5–10 minutes. Lift out carefully with a fork and allow to cool.

EF; DF; GF; WF | Makes 12

TIP: The batter for these and the tomato polenta muffins (see opposite page) can be made in advance and left in the fridge overnight until ready to bake.

Tomato polenta 'muffins'

Tomato polenta 'muffins'

3 cups water
1 cup polenta
1 Tbsp olive oil
¼ tsp salt

6 cherry tomatoes, halved
herb salt and ground black pepper to taste
extra olive oil for drizzling

1. Preheat the oven to 180 °C. Spray a muffin pan with non-stick cooking spray.
2. Bring the water to the boil in a pot and add the polenta, oil and salt. Stir until it thickens to a porridge-like consistency, then ladle into the muffin pan. Leave to cool to allow the polenta to 'set'.
3. Press a cherry tomato half, cut-side up, into the top of each muffin. Drizzle a little olive oil over each and sprinkle with the salt and pepper. Bake for 30–40 minutes until the muffins pull away from the sides of the pan. Remove from the oven and leave to stand for 5–10 minutes. Lift out carefully with a fork and allow to cool. These make a delicious snack or side dish with a meat meal.

EF; DF; NF; GF; WF; SF | Makes 12

SNACK KEBABS

Traditionally, the term 'kebab' refers to skewered meats and/or vegetables cooked either over a hot flame or under a grill. However, one can also thread a selection of raw fruits and/or cheeses onto a wooden skewer.

Fruit kebabs

½ pineapple, peeled and cored
2 mangoes, peeled, halved and stoned
1 melon, peeled, halved and deseeded
2 kiwi fruit, peeled and quartered
12 litchis, peeled, halved and stoned

¼ watermelon, deseeded
6 strawberries
6 figs, quartered
12 sprigs of fresh mint, washed
6 wooden kebab skewers

1. Choose 4–6 different types of fruit from the list above.
2. Cut the fruits into rough shapes and thread onto the wooden skewers, alternating every third fruit with a sprig of mint. Chill until required, and serve drizzled with honey or a yoghurt dip.

EF; DF; GF; WF; NF; SF | Makes 6

Grilled vegetable kebabs

3 Tbsp olive oil
2 Tbsp balsamic vinegar
1 Tbsp lemon juice
1 Tbsp Dijon mustard
1 Tbsp chopped fresh parsley
1 clove garlic, minced
freshly ground black pepper to taste

1 red onion, peeled and quartered
  (separate the layers)
1 red pepper, deseeded and cut into 8
1 yellow pepper, deseeded and cut into 8
2 baby marrows, each cut into 4 pieces
8 button mushrooms, stems removed
4 wooden kebab skewers, soaked in water

1. Mix the oil, vinegar, lemon juice, mustard, parsley, garlic and pepper in a large Ziploc™ bag. Add the vegetables and toss. Refrigerate for 2–3 hours.
2. Preheat the oven to grill at 200 °C. Place the vegetables on the skewers, alternating as you go. Keep the marinade to brush over the vegetables as they cook.
3. Grill for 10–15 minutes, brushing with the marinade every 3–4 minutes. Remove from the grill when the vegetables are brown and tender. Serve on their own or as a side dish with braaied meat, fish or chicken.

EF; DF; GF; WF; NF; SF | Makes 4

Fruit kebabs

Olive & feta kebab snacks

3 Tbsp olive oil
2 Tbsp lemon juice
1 tsp dried rosemary
½ tsp salt
freshly ground black pepper to taste
2–3 wheels feta, cubed

1 x 400 g jar pitted Calamata olives
1 English cucumber, sliced into thick discs
1 red pepper, deseeded and cut into 8
1 x 400 g punnet cherry tomatoes
8 wooden kebab skewers

1. Whisk together the oil, lemon juice, rosemary, salt and pepper and set aside.
2. Thread the feta, olives and vegetables onto the wooden skewers, alternating as you go.
3. Drizzle with the dressing and serve on a side plate.

EF; GF; WF; NF | Makes 8

Popcorn treat variations

1 cup popcorn
little sunflower oil

toppings of your choice

1. Make the popcorn in an air or microwave popper or on the stove top with a little sunflower oil.
2. Fill individual, small, brown paper packets or small bowls with the popcorn and try the following variations:

Savoury: Drizzle with olive oil and sprinkle liberally with Ina Paarman's Herb and Garlic Salt.
Sweet: Sift over 1 heaped tsp caster sugar per portion.
Decadent: Add a small knob of butter followed by caster sugar.
Caramelised: In a small pot over a medium heat, melt 1 cup sugar, stirring continuously. Add 1 Tbsp butter. When melted, pour over the popcorn, toss with a spoon and allow to cool before eating. Hot sugar burns!

EF; DF; WF; GF; NF | Serves 4

When having a smackerel of something with a friend, don't eat
so much that you get stuck in the doorway trying to get out.

Anon, *Pooh's Little Book of Wisdom*

Easy trail mix

½ cup sesame seeds
1 cup sunflower seeds
1 cup pumpkin seeds
¼ cup linseeds/flax seeds (optional)

1 cup raw almonds (optional)
1 cup seedless raisins
1 cup dried cranberries
1 cup chopped dried mango/pear/apricot

1. Combine all of the ingredients and store in an airtight container.
2. This makes a healthy school, work, party, beach and hiking snack.

EF; DF; WF; GF; alt NF | Makes 12 portions of ½ cup each

Ants on a log

celery stalks, rinsed and dried
Filling (choose ONE of these for your diet)
peanut or soy butter
almond or cashew butter
cream, cottage or goat's cheese
hummus or guacamole

Ants (choose for your diet)
raisins or currants
dried sweetened cranberries
dried blueberries
walnuts, almonds or pecan nuts
sunflower or pumpkin seeds

1. Fill the celery sticks with a filling of your choice.
2. Sprinkle with the 'ants' and serve at children's birthday parties.

WF; EF; GF; alt DF; alt NF | Make as many as you need

Kiddies banana pops

2 wooden kebab skewers
1 ripe, firm banana, cut in half
honey or melted dairy-free chocolate

crushed nuts, sunflower/pumpkin/sesame
seeds, desiccated coconut, etc.

1. Roll the banana halves in honey or dip in melted dairy-free chocolate.
2. According to your allergies, sprinkle with either crushed nuts, seeds, desiccated coconut, etc.

EF; WF; GF; DF; alt NF | Serves 2

Apple & mint
iced tea (page 137)

Since the human body tends to move in the direction of its expectations – plus or minus – it is important to know that attitudes of confidence and determination are no less a part of the treatment program than medical and science technology.

Norman Cousin

Miscellaneous

For those of you who struggle with preservatives, read on. In the words of my son Lennie, this is the 'lotions and potions' section – the fun and funky experiments that are just too cool and fun to leave out and are easy and cost effective to make. The iced tea, lemonade and ginger beer are excellent for when entertaining guests … try them!

Aroma cream

When we lived in Seattle, before Sam was born, I used to make a product called 'Len & Joe's aroma dough'. I use the same oils to make this cream. It's excellent for sensitive skins. For skin sensitive to colouring, omit the food colouring and instead use vegetable colouring, e.g. beet juice or carrot juice reduction.

1 x 500 ml tub Aqueous cream
10–12 drops essential oil

¼ tsp food colouring of your choice

1. Drop the essential oil and food colouring directly into the tub of Aqueous cream. To achieve different scents, see below. Blend well with a spoon.

Blue: Mix 4 drops Roman chamomile and 6–8 drops mandarin oil with ¼ tsp blue food colouring – the scent is fresh and the effect calming, soothing and brightening.
Green: Mix 4 drops grapefruit, 4 drops eucalyptus and 4 drops peppermint oil with ¼ tsp green food colouring – the effect is anti-viral, decongesting and joyful.
Lavender: Mix 6 drops lavender and 4 drops Roman chamomile oil with ⅛ tsp red and ⅛ tsp blue food colouring – this is for quiet play and sweet dreams, and is great for a bedtime massage after the bath.
Orange: Mix 10 drops orange oil (or 4 drops neroli and 8 drops mandarin oil) with ¼ tsp orange food colouring – the effect is brightening, bringing a little sun on a rainy day.
Pink: Mix 10 drops geranium oil with ¼ tsp rose-pink food colouring – the scent is floral and the effect is comforting and anti-depressant.
Yellow: Mix 8 drops grapefruit and 4 drops lemongrass oil with ¼ tsp yellow food colouring – the effect is joyful and inspiring, and enhances creative focus.

Bath salts

1 cup Epsom salts
1 cup sea salt or kosher salt
1–2 tsp glycerin
10–12 drops essential oil of your choice
   (e.g. lavender oil)

½ tsp food colouring of your choice
   (e.g. purple) or 2 tsp vegetable colouring
   (e.g. beet juice)
¼ –½ cup rose petals or lavender flowers

1. In a medium-sized bowl, mix all of the ingredients.
2. Spoon into a clean, dry jar and use ½ cup per bath.
3. As an example of an alternative, you can substitute rosemary leaves for the petals and use rosemary oil with green food colouring.

Eczema tea bath

This works well for dry, irritated excema or winter skin. It soothes and heals the skin and has a pleasant aroma.

5–6 rooibos tea bags	boiling water

1. Place the tea bags in a large jug or tea pot and pour over the boiling water. Allow to steep for 5–10 minutes. Remove the tea bags and pour this into your bath water. Soak for 10–15 minutes.

Apple & mint iced tea

2 mint tea bags	½ apple, unpeeled and sliced
2 rooibos tea bags	2 sprigs of fresh mint
3 cups boiling water	ice cubes and cold water
1 cup apple juice	honey or sugar to taste (optional)

1. In a large glass jug, steep the tea bags in the boiling water for 10 minutes. Remove the tea bags and add the apple juice, apple slices and mint sprigs.
2. Top up with ice cubes and cold water. Add honey or sugar to taste if you prefer your iced tea sweeter. Refrigerate until needed. This keeps in the fridge for 2 days.

DF; EF; GF; WF; NF; alt SF | Makes 1 litre

Ginger beer

4 litres water	1 tsp dry yeast (brewer's yeast)
4 cups sugar	1 Tbsp seedless raisins
30 g root ginger, mashed with a mallet	

1. Boil the water in a pot and add the sugar and mashed ginger root. Simmer for 10 minutes, then remove from the heat and cool until lukewarm.
2. Add the yeast and leave the pot with the lid on slightly skew for 2 days. Stir at the end of the first day.
3. The mixture will smell strongly of yeast and fermentation. Strain, add the raisins and bottle in screw-top bottles, not corked bottles as the pressure will pop the cork right out. Chill and serve. It keeps in the fridge for up to 10 days.

DF; EF; GF; NF; WF | Makes about 4 litres

Lemonade

6 large lemons
1½ cups white sugar
1 cup water

about 1 litre soda water
ice cubes
sprigs of mint for decoration

1. Wash the lemons, then grate the zest off 2 of them. Squeeze the juice from all the lemons and strain.
2. Add the sugar to the water in a medium-sized pot and stir in the lemon zest. Bring to the boil, stirring to dissolve the sugar, then simmer for 10 minutes. Set aside to cool.
3. Stir in the strained lemon juice and pour into a clean glass bottle.
4. To serve, use 1 part lemon syrup to 2 parts soda water. Add lots of ice cubes and a sprig of mint for decoration.

DF; EF; GF; NF; WF | Serves 4–6

Almond milk

Almond milk is high in calcium. The benefit of homemade almond milk is that it has no additives or preservatives and you can control the amount of sweetness.

1 cup raw almonds
4 cups filtered water

4 fresh pitted dates or 2 Tbsp honey

1. Soak the almonds in water for at least 6 hours or overnight if possible. Drain and place the almonds in a blender with the 4 cups of fresh filtered water. Blend until you get a milk-like consistency.
2. If you like a hint of sweetness, blend in the dates or honey. Now strain the milk to remove the granules. The result is a delicious, creamy milk. Store in a sealed glass jar or covered jug.
3. Drink it plain, use in coffee or tea or pour over cereal. It will keep in the fridge for 4–5 days.

DF; EF; GF; WF | Makes 1 litre

Aroma dough play-dough

This play-dough is a great stress reliever. Note that although this is made from edible ingredients and is not toxic in small amounts, it is not intended as a food item. Please be sure to put it away after your children have finished playing. You will need a mixer for this recipe.

2 cups boiling water or rooibos tea
1 Tbsp oil
1 tsp food colouring or
    1 Tbsp vegetable colouring
2 cups flour

1 Tbsp cream of tartar
½ tsp glycerin (optional)
6–8 drops essential oils of your choice
1 cup salt

1. Pour the boiling water or tea, oil, food colouring and 1 cup of the flour into the bowl of a mixer. Using a dough hook, start blending on a slow speed.
2. Add the cream of tartar, glycerin (if using) and essential oils, and blend again. Add the salt and remaining flour, ½ cup at a time. Continue blending until the dough comes together and is smooth. Remove from the bowl and allow to cool before refrigerating.
3. Store in the fridge in a sealed plastic container as it contains no preservatives. It should last 1–2 months.

Furniture polish

Furniture polish and other spray cleaners are an irritant to people who suffer from allergies or asthma. So here is the solution. This one doesn't make me sneeze, wheeze or cough.

1 Tbsp olive oil
1 Tbsp lemon juice

2 drops lemongrass or mint essential oil

1. Combine all of the ingredients in a spray bottle.
2. Spray onto wooden furniture sparingly and polish off.

Shopping list

Photocopy this list and take it with you next time you go grocery shopping. On it, you will find all the ingredients used in this book.

BAKING
- ❑ baking powder
- ❑ bicarbonate of soda
- ❑ carob
- ❑ chocolate chips
- ❑ chocolate sprinkles/curls
- ❑ cocoa powder
- ❑ cooking chocolate (dark and milk)
- ❑ custard powder
- ❑ dry yeast (instant and active)
- ❑ eggs
- ❑ food colouring
- ❑ Orgran No Egg powder
- ❑ vanilla essence
- ❑ xanthan gum

BEVERAGE ITEMS
- ❑ apple juice
- ❑ Appletizer™
- ❑ beer
- ❑ instant coffee
- ❑ lemon juice
- ❑ lime juice
- ❑ mint tea bags
- ❑ orange juice
- ❑ peach juice
- ❑ rooibos tea bags
- ❑ soda water
- ❑ sparkling wine
- ❑ white wine

BREADS
- ❑ French loaf
- ❑ rye bread

CANNED GOODS
- ❑ baked beans
- ❑ beetroot
- ❑ black cherries
- ❑ black olives
- ❑ butter beans
- ❑ Calamata olives
- ❑ chickpeas
- ❑ chopped peeled tomatoes
- ❑ creamstyle sweetcorn
- ❑ cucumber
- ❑ fruit cocktail
- ❑ green olives
- ❑ jack mackerel
- ❑ kidney beans
- ❑ mandarin orange segments
- ❑ peach halves
- ❑ peach slices
- ❑ pears
- ❑ peppadews
- ❑ pickled cucumbers
- ❑ pineapple pieces
- ❑ pineapple rings
- ❑ sugar beans
- ❑ sundried tomatoes
- ❑ tomato soup
- ❑ tuna

CEREALS
- ❑ cornflakes
- ❑ Jungle oats
- ❑ Maltabella
- ❑ oat bran
- ❑ Oatees
- ❑ oats
- ❑ original wheat-free Pronutro
- ❑ Rice Krispies
- ❑ rolled oats

CHEESE
- ❑ blue cheese
- ❑ Brie cheese
- ❑ Camembert cheese
- ❑ Cheddar cheese
- ❑ feta cheese
- ❑ goat's milk cheese (log chevin)
- ❑ mozzarella cheese
- ❑ Parmesan cheese

CONDIMENTS AND SAUCES
- ❑ apple sauce
- ❑ chilli sauce
- ❑ chutney
- ❑ mayonnaise (egg-free or tangy)
- ❑ soy sauce
- ❑ Tabasco
- ❑ tamari
- ❑ tomato sauce
- ❑ wasabi
- ❑ Worcestershire sauce

CREAM
- ❑ Orley Whip™ non-dairy cream
- ❑ pouring cream
- ❑ sour cream
- ❑ soy cream
- ❑ whipping cream

FATS AND OILS
- ❑ butter
- ❑ canola oil
- ❑ dairy-free margarine
- ❑ olive oil
- ❑ peanut oil
- ❑ sesame oil
- ❑ sunflower oil
- ❑ vegetable oil

FLOURS
- ❑ all-purpose flour
- ❑ almond meal
- ❑ barley flour
- ❑ brown rice flour
- ❑ buckwheat flour
- ❑ cake flour
- ❑ coconut flour
- ❑ fine rye flour
- ❑ matzo meal
- ❑ millet flour
- ❑ Nutty Wheat flour
- ❑ oat flour
- ❑ potato flour
- ❑ potato starch
- ❑ rolled oats
- ❑ self-raising flour
- ❑ sorghum meal
- ❑ soya flour
- ❑ stoneground rye flour
- ❑ tapioca flour
- ❑ wheat bread flour
- ❑ white bread flour
- ❑ white maize meal
- ❑ white rice flour
- ❑ wholewheat flour
- ❑ yellow maize meal
- ❑ yellow polenta meal

FRUIT
- ❑ apricots (dried)
- ❑ avocados
- ❑ baby tomatoes
- ❑ bananas
- ❑ blueberries
- ❑ cantaloupe (spanspek)
- ❑ cherry tomatoes
- ❑ cranberries (dried)
- ❑ currants
- ❑ dried fruit (apple, mango, pear, apricot, etc.)
- ❑ figs
- ❑ frozen berries
- ❑ goji berries (dried)
- ❑ Golden Delicious apples
- ❑ Granny Smith apples
- ❑ green seedless grapes
- ❑ honeydew melon
- ❑ kiwi fruit
- ❑ lemons
- ❑ litchis
- ❑ mangoes
- ❑ nectarines
- ❑ oranges
- ❑ pears
- ❑ pineapple
- ❑ pitted dates
- ❑ raspberries
- ❑ red apples
- ❑ roma tomatoes

- ❏ seedless raisins
- ❏ strawberries
- ❏ watermelon

HERBS AND SPICES
- ❏ basil leaves
- ❏ bay leaves
- ❏ cayenne pepper
- ❏ chillies
- ❏ cloves
- ❏ coriander
- ❏ crushed garlic
- ❏ cumin
- ❏ curry powder
- ❏ dill
- ❏ dried granulated garlic
- ❏ dried origanum
- ❏ dried sage
- ❏ dried thyme
- ❏ fennel
- ❏ ginger root
- ❏ ground allspice
- ❏ ground black pepper
- ❏ ground cinnamon
- ❏ ground ginger
- ❏ herb salt
- ❏ Herbamare® Organic Herb Seasoning Salt
- ❏ Ina Paarman's Garlic and Herb Salt
- ❏ Ina Paarman's Garlic Pepper Seasoning
- ❏ Ina Paarman's Green Onion Seasoning
- ❏ Ina Paarman's Seasoned Sea Salt or sea salt flakes
- ❏ kosher salt
- ❏ mint leaves
- ❏ paprika
- ❏ parsley
- ❏ peppercorns
- ❏ plain salt
- ❏ rosemary
- ❏ turmeric

MEAT
- ❏ beef mince
- ❏ chicken breasts
- ❏ chicken pieces
- ❏ lamb mince
- ❏ minute steaks

- ❏ stewing lamb
- ❏ whole chicken

MILK
- ❏ almond milk
- ❏ buttermilk
- ❏ coconut milk
- ❏ cow's milk
- ❏ cow's milk powder
- ❏ goat's milk
- ❏ rice milk
- ❏ rice milk powder
- ❏ soy milk
- ❏ soy milk powder

MISCELLANEOUS
- ❏ desiccated coconut
- ❏ dried pomegranate arils
- ❏ Ina Paarman's Sundried Tomato Pesto
- ❏ nori
- ❏ peach jelly
- ❏ peanut brittle
- ❏ popcorn
- ❏ smoked tofu
- ❏ tomato paste
- ❏ tomato purée
- ❏ wooden kebab skewers

MUSTARDS
- ❏ Dijon
- ❏ powdered
- ❏ prepared

NUTS
- ❏ almonds
- ❏ cashew nuts
- ❏ flaked almonds
- ❏ pecan nuts
- ❏ pine nuts
- ❏ walnuts

PULSES AND GRAINS
- ❏ arborio rice
- ❏ basmati rice
- ❏ brown lentils
- ❏ brown rice
- ❏ buckwheat
- ❏ corn and rice pasta (fettuccine/fusilli/penne)
- ❏ couscous

- ❏ durum wheat pasta (fettuccine/fusilli/penne)
- ❏ pearl barley
- ❏ polenta
- ❏ quinoa
- ❏ red lentils
- ❏ rice noodles
- ❏ split peas
- ❏ sushi rice
- ❏ wheat- or gluten-free macaroni
- ❏ white rice

SEAFOOD
- ❏ Cape salmon
- ❏ smoked salmon
- ❏ yellowtail

SEEDS
- ❏ flax/linseeds
- ❏ poppy seeds
- ❏ pumpkin seeds
- ❏ sesame seeds
- ❏ sunflower seeds

SPREADS
- ❏ Golden syrup
- ❏ honey
- ❏ hummus
- ❏ raspberry jam
- ❏ smooth apricot jam
- ❏ smooth peanut butter
- ❏ tahini

STOCKS
- ❏ chicken stock cubes
- ❏ Ina Paarman's Chicken Stock Powder
- ❏ Ina Paarman's Vegetable Stock Powder
- ❏ vegetable stock cubes

SUGAR AND SUGAR SUBSTITUTES
- ❏ brown sugar
- ❏ caster sugar
- ❏ dark brown sugar
- ❏ fructose
- ❏ icing sugar
- ❏ organic cane sugar
- ❏ stevia

- ❏ white sugar
- ❏ xylitol

VEGETABLES
- ❏ baby marrows
- ❏ baby potatoes
- ❏ broccoli
- ❏ butternut
- ❏ button mushrooms
- ❏ cabbage
- ❏ carrots
- ❏ cauliflower
- ❏ celery
- ❏ chives
- ❏ English cucumber
- ❏ frozen corn kernels
- ❏ frozen green beans
- ❏ frozen mixed vegetables
- ❏ frozen peas
- ❏ garlic
- ❏ green beans
- ❏ green peppers
- ❏ leeks
- ❏ lettuce leaves
- ❏ mushrooms
- ❏ potatoes
- ❏ purple onions
- ❏ red onions
- ❏ red peppers
- ❏ rocket leaves
- ❏ spinach
- ❏ spring onions
- ❏ sweet potatoes
- ❏ turnips
- ❏ white onions
- ❏ yellow peppers

VINEGARS
- ❏ apple cider vinegar
- ❏ balsamic vinegar
- ❏ Japanese rice vinegar
- ❏ red wine vinegar
- ❏ white vinegar

YOGHURT
- ❏ fruit flavoured yoghurt
- ❏ plain yoghurt
- ❏ vanilla yoghurt

Index

Page numbers in bold indicate photographs.

If ever there is tomorrow when we're not together … there is something you must always remember.
You are braver than you believe, stronger than you seem and smarter than you think.
But the most important thing is, even if we're apart … I'll always be with you.

A.A. Milne, *Winnie the Pooh*